Lenses on Composition Studies

Series Editors, Sheryl Fontaine and Steve Westbrook

LENSES ON COMPOSITION STUDIES
Series Editors, Sheryl Fontaine and Steve Westbrook

Lenses on Composition Studies offers authors the unique opportunity to write for advanced undergraduate and beginning graduate students who are new to the discipline of Composition Studies. While the series aims to maintain the rigor and depth of contemporary composition scholarship, it seeks to offer this particular group of students an introduction to key disciplinary issues in accessible prose that does not assume prior advanced knowledge of scholars and theoretical debates. The series provides instructors of advanced undergraduate or beginning graduate students texts that are both appropriate and inviting for this fresh but professionally directed audience.

Bibliographic Research in Composition Studies

Vicki Byard

Parlor Press
West Lafayette, Indiana
www.parlorpress.com

Parlor Press LLC, West Lafayette, Indiana 47906

Printed in the United States of America

SAN: 254-8879

Library of Congress Cataloging-in-Publication Data

Byard, Vicki, 1961-
  Bibliographic research in composition studies / Vicki Byard.
      p. cm. -- (Lenses on composition studies)
  Includes bibliographical references and indexes.
  ISBN 978-1-60235-131-8 (pbk. : alk. paper) -- ISBN 978-1-60235-132-5
(alk. paper) -- ISBN 978-1-60235-133-2 (adobe ebook : alk. paper)
  1. English language--Rhetoric--Study and teaching. 2. English language--
Rhetoric--Research--Methodology. I. Title.
  PE1404.B93 2009
  808'.04207--dc22
                                    2009036437

This book is printed on acid-free paper.

Parlor Press, LLC is an independent publisher of scholarly and trade titles
in print and multimedia formats. This book is available in paperback, cloth,
and Adobe eBook formats from Parlor Press on the World Wide Web at
http://www.parlorpress.com. For submission information or to find out about
Parlor Press publications, write to Parlor Press, 816 Robinson St., West Lafayette, Indiana, 47906, or e-mail editor@parlorpress.com.

Contents

Bibliographic Research in Composition Studies

1 Directions to the Parlor: The Need for a Guide to Scholarship in Composition Studies

The publisher of this book, Parlor Press, derives its name from a frequently quoted passage by theorist Kenneth Burke, a passage especially relevant to this text's mission of guiding readers to a discipline's scholarship:

> Imagine that you enter a parlor. You come late. When you arrive, others have long preceded you, and they are engaged in a heated discussion, a discussion too heated for them to pause and tell you exactly what it is about. In fact, the discussion had already begun long before any of them got there, so that no one present is qualified to retrace for you all the steps that had gone before. You listen for a while, until you decide that you have caught the tenor of the argument; then you put in your oar. Someone answers; you answer him; another comes to your defense; another aligns himself against you, to either the embarrassment or gratification of your opponent, depending upon the quality of your ally's assistance. However, the discussion is interminable. The hour grows late, you must depart. And you do depart, with the discussion still vigorously in progress. (110–11)

Although Burke used this metaphor to describe the drama of human existence—you enter the parlor at your birth, mature to participate in the "unending conversation" of civilization, and then exit the parlor upon your death—the passage is sometimes quoted in composition scholarship as an apt description of how knowledge is constructed in an academic discipline. When a student or other newcomer first encounters a discipline, she finds its scholars engaged in an intense conversation that has been evolving since the discipline's inception. If the student is intrigued by the conversation taking place, she listens—she studies it—until she is informed enough to join the conversation herself as a publishing scholar. Consistent with Burke's metaphor, the conversation of a discipline—its scholarship—continues beyond any one individual's participation.

Gary Olson is one composition specialist who has written explicitly about the correlation between an ongoing conversation and scholarship in composition studies. In his essay "Publishing Scholarship in Rhetoric and Composition: Joining the Conversation," Olson depicts a scene quite similar to Burke's metaphor of a parlor conversation:

> [I]magine a faculty cocktail party in which various colleagues and their spouses are standing in groups sipping cocktails and engaging in intimate, sometimes passionate discussions. After freshening your cocktail, you approach several people discussing the influence of postmodern theory on composition pedagogy. Obviously, it would be considered rude to jump immediately into the conversation that had been going on before you arrived. Basic etiquette dictates that you join the group, quietly listen to what is being said, and develop a sense of the larger conversation—both its tone and content—before you begin to make a contribution. The same kind of dynamics attend to the scholarly conversation. Before rushing into print about this or that subject, it is imperative that you read what is currently being said about the subject, discover what the positions are and who is taking what position, and in general, acquire a sense of the larger conversation. (21)

In quoting both Burke and Olson at length, I invite you to imagine the scholarship of composition studies as a lively conversation that is well underway. Is this a conversation you would like to listen to and perhaps eventually join? If so, this book will aid you by providing directions for finding the composition studies' parlor, that is, the books, journals, and other sites where the scholarly conversations of this discipline are taking place. In writing this guide, I hope to both ease and speed your entry into this scholarly conversation.

For Writing and Discussion

1. If the scholarship of composition studies can be aptly described as a conversation taking place in a parlor, what experiences have led you to the doorway of this parlor? Why are you interested in stepping inside to hear the conversation?

2. Suppose that you are interested in reading more about composition studies but can't now imagine that you might join the conversation by publishing in the future. What value might you still find in simply listening to the conversation for a while?

THE NEED FOR STUDENT-CENTERED INTRODUCTIONS TO COMPOSITION STUDIES

Guides written specifically to introduce advanced undergraduates and beginning graduate students to the discipline of composition studies, such as this text, are only now beginning to be published. One reason is because composition studies emerged as a discipline relatively recently. In his article "Composition History and Disciplinarity," Robert Connors states that "we can trace the possibility of the field of composition studies" (8) from the New Rhetoric of the 1960s, but that "the founding decade of the disciplinarity of composition studies" (8) was the 1970s, the decade when much serious scholarship in rhetoric and composition began to be published and when the first rhetoric doctoral programs in English departments were formed. However, it wasn't until the 1980s, writes Connors, that composition studies experienced the "full-blown growth of disciplinarity" (10).

Since then, the composition studies parlor has become increasingly populated with students. According to surveys published periodically in the journal *Rhetoric Review* (see Chapman and Tate; Brown et al.), there were 38 composition doctoral programs in 1986 and 72 such programs when the survey was updated in 1993, a near doubling of programs in just seven years. Though the number of doctoral programs declined slightly to 65 by the next survey of programs, conducted in 1999, the total enrollment of students in composition doctoral programs had increased by ten percent, up to 1,276. The first survey of MA programs in composition studies, conducted in 2004, identified 55 programs, yet the authors of this survey admit the likelihood that many MA programs in rhetoric and composition were not represented in this survey.

As student enrollments in composition studies programs have grown, so too have compositionists' discussions about how to best prepare students for entry to the discipline. For example, Louise Wetherbee Phelps has argued for the development of a graduate writing pedagogy, one that faculty can use "in teaching graduate students as prospective scholars how to engage in a postmodern rhetoric" (67). Janice Lauer has raised questions about whether students should be expected to become active members of the profession, even to publish, while they are still in graduate school. Karen Peirce and Theresa Enos have expressed concern that faculty who teach in graduate composition programs share little consensus about graduate curricula, including what kinds of writing assignments are required and what textbooks are used.

The issue of how best to facilitate students entering the conversation of composition studies is addressed most recently and comprehensively in the 2006 book *Culture Shock and the Practice of Profession: Training the New Wave in Rhetoric & Composition*, edited by Virginia Anderson and Susan Romano. In one essay from this volume, "Inviting Students into Composition Studies with a New Instructional Genre," Sheryl Fontaine and Susan Hunter critique the "immersion approach to instruction" (198) that has been a mainstay of composition studies programs, whereby "students are expected to jump into the middle of the stream of expert-level discussions and, through a sink-or-swim process, come to understand the various arguments and their relation to one another" (198). Fontaine and Hunter argue that this approach, which may have questionable merit in any discipline, is particularly unsuitable for composition studies because nearly all students entering graduate composition programs have had little or no introduction to the discipline as undergraduates. Thus, students have no "knowledge-building schema" (203), no ready framework for judging the relative importance of what they read or context for interpreting the issues at stake. Fontaine and Hunter then build a case for a new instructional genre in composition studies, books that are written specifically for students entering the discipline, that "acknowledge [students'] position at the threshold of disciplinary knowledge and would actually prepare them to become expert learners in the field of Composition" (203). Such texts, say Fontaine and Hunter, should aim to teach students "the behaviors and practices of the discipline" (206) and should present "theoretical or practical concepts and methods of inquiry that could cross courses" (207), reflecting a "curricula whose rhythms draw on habits of mind much more than the replication of expert knowledge" (207).

To meet the need for texts in this new instructional genre, Parlor Press created the Lenses on Composition Studies series, and this is the first text to be published in the series. As a student beginning your training in composition studies, you're crossing the threshold into the disciplinary parlor at an especially opportune time. As scholars in the discipline, we welcome you. We hope to make you more comfortable while you listen for a while, so when you're ready you may join us in the conversation.

For Writing and Discussion

1. As a student beginning to learn about composition studies, what do (or did) you find challenging about reading scholarship in the discipline?

2. Prior to picking up this book, what, if anything, has helped to ease your entry to the composition studies parlor?

THE NEED FOR BIBLIOGRAPHIC INSTRUCTION IN ACADEMIA

In addition to answering a call for more student-centered introductions to composition studies, this book also answers a call from academic librarians for bibliographic instruction to be integrated into courses in the disciplines. Bibliographic instruction emerged as a distinct field for academic librarians, coincidentally, during the same period that composition studies was developing as a discipline (Fister, "Common Ground"). According to librarian Larry Hardesty, the modern period of attention to bibliographic instruction began in 1969 and "by the early 1970s, bibliographic instruction had emerged as an authentic movement" (340). In 1983, a scholarly journal devoted to the field was initiated, entitled *Research Strategies*. Shortly afterwards, bibliographic instruction became a priority of the Association of College &

Research Libraries (ACRL), which is the major professional organization of academic libraries and is a division of the American Library Association (ALA). In 1987, the ACRL developed its first "Model Statement of Objectives for Academic Bibliographic Instruction." As library resources became more prevalent online, librarians began to replace the term "bibliographic instruction" with the more comprehensive term "information literacy." The ACRL then issued two additional documents meant to advance such instruction: "Information Literacy Competency Standards for Higher Education," approved in 2000, and "Objectives for Information Literacy Instruction: A Model Statement for Academic Librarians," approved in 2001 as a revision of the ACRL's earlier model statement of objectives for bibliographic instruction.

Bibliographic instruction, especially when defined more broadly as information literacy, trains students to do much more than locate relevant sources. The skills that comprise information literacy are best delineated in the following excerpt from the ACRL's document "Information Literacy Competency Standards for Higher Education":

An information literate individual is able to:

- Determine the extent of information needed
- Access the needed information effectively and efficiently
- Evaluate information and its sources critically
- Incorporate selected information into one's knowledge base
- Use information effectively to accomplish a specific purpose
- Understand the economic, legal, and social issues surrounding the use of information, and access and use information ethically and legally

Librarians hope that information literacy skills will be introduced to students in elementary and secondary schools, and that information literacy instruction and practice will be incorporated more fully into the higher education curriculum in all disciplines and at all levels, including graduate courses (Rockman). Such in-depth instruction is all the more necessary because in recent decades, academic libraries have undergone radical changes, largely because of technological developments. Not long ago, students and scholars who wished to research a topic needed to spend long hours physically in the library, sifting by hand through a card catalogue and annual bound volumes that indexed journal articles. Now, much research can be conducted from outside the walls of the library, through online catalogues and databases that allow users to conduct far more exhaustive searches and to do so far more quickly. Such ease in searching presents students with new challenges. As librarian Ilene Rockman explains, "the issue is no longer one of not having enough information; it is just the opposite—too much information, in various formats and not all of equal value" (1). Given such wealth of information, continues Rockman, "the ability to act confidently (and not be paralyzed by information overload) is critical to academic success and personal self-directed learning" (1).

Librarians are also adamant that bibliographic instruction be integrated into courses, not addressed solely by librarians in one or two class sessions. As Patricia Senn Breivik, past President of the ACRL and Chair of the National Forum on Information Literacy, states succinctly, "information literacy is a learning issue not a library issue" (xii). For this reason, librarians have expressed interest in forming more collaborative partnerships with faculty. For example, librarian Larry Hardesty has analyzed faculty culture to determine why faculty resist bibliographic instruction in their courses. After determining that the biggest obstacles to this instruction are faculty's sense of inadequate instructional time and faculty's reluctance to view librarians as peers, he concludes that librarians must take the initiative in forging better relationships with faculty through one-on-one informal contacts and through publishing about information literacy in sources that are likely to be read by faculty in the disciplines. Also, as recently as 2004, in an essay entitled "Developing Faculty-Librarian Partnerships in Information Literacy," Susan Carol Curzon coaches librarians on how to interest faculty in the need for student information literacy skills. She advises librarians to relate information literacy to critical thinking, which faculty value already; to discuss information literacy as a lifelong skill; to talk about how information literacy helps students succeed academically; to stress that information literacy is an essential skill in academic life; and to present faculty with data that assesses students' current information literacy skills.

Perhaps the strongest argument for course-integrated bibliographic instruction is that it improves students' academic work, as confirmed in an empirical study conducted by librarians David Kohl and Lizabeth Wilson. Based on their study's data, Kohl and Wilson conclude that "bibliographic instruction taught as a cognitive strategy did increase the quality of student bibliographies to a statistically significant degree" (209). Although their study was published in 1986, prior to the ACRL's rich articulation of information literacy I have cited above, their qualification that the approach must be "taught as a cognitive strategy" is fully consistent with more contemporary definitions of information literacy. The effectiveness of course-integrated information literacy can be deduced from their discussion of their conclusions:

> The traditional, tool-specific approach does not seem as helpful as an approach that focuses on helping students develop a more complex, appropriate, and individualized research strategy for themselves. [. . .] If bibliographic instruction is to be effective, it needs to be recast into an approach that begins with the student's research question rather than the library tool and that focuses on understanding how information is organized rather than simply explaining the mechanics of how to use library tools. (210).

My hope is that the bibliographic skills you learn from this book will not only help you to complete a specific assignment for a course in composition studies but will also increase your information literacy skills more generally, making you more equipped for any research endeavor you undertake.

For Writing and Discussion

1. In commenting on the ease of online bibliographic searches, librarian Ilene Rockman writes that it is easy for students to be "paralyzed by information overload" (1). Have you ever felt paralyzed by too much information when working on an academic assignment?

   a. If you have felt paralyzed in this way, describe the experience. Then review the ACRL's bulleted list of skills that characterize a person with information literacy, cited earlier in this chapter. Which of these skills do you think would most have helped you resolve this paralysis? How so?

b. If you cannot remember feeling paralyzed by information overload, describe any prior bibliographic instruction you have received that you think has helped you to avoid this experience. Then review the ACRL's bulleted list of skills that characterize a person with information literacy, cited earlier in this chapter. Which of these skills are strengths you developed from your previous bibliographic instruction? Which of these skills do you still hope to improve?

2. Identify someone who has been employed as either a faculty member or an academic librarian for at least ten years. Informally interview this person about how technological developments in the last decade have changed the process they use when searching for academic sources. Summarize the person's responses; then describe what this interview exercise has taught you about the merits and the limitations of bibliographic instruction.

The Need for Bibliographic Instruction in Composition Studies

We have just examined the need for bibliographic instruction in all academic disciplines; in this section we will examine why bibliographic instruction is particularly necessary in composition studies.

Although he was not the first to call for bibliographic rigor in composition studies, the person who is most often credited with initiating a demand for bibliographic resources in the discipline is Paul Bryant, 1973 chair of the Conference on College Composition and Communication (CCCC) and the first to chair the CCCC Commission on a Bibliography for the Profession in 1981. In his keynote address as CCCC chair, entitled "A Brand New World Every Morning," Bryant lamented that the teaching of composition at the time was notably ill-informed by earlier scholarship. Without an annual bibliography on teaching composition, wrote Bryant, the discipline was ahistorical, like a brand new world every morning, one that permitted "the repeated reinvention of the same pedagogical wheels" (30), which Bryant bluntly described as "wasteful and stupid, to say the least" (31). It is only through a greater awareness of work already done, he wrote, that the discipline can develop in ways that are "as linearly progressive as possible" (32).

Yet several characteristics make composition studies challenging for bibliographers to manage. According to Patrick Scott, who has written extensively about bibliographic problems in composition studies, one of the greatest challenges is the classification of subjects. Unlike scholarship about literature, which can be classified almost entirely using proper names, such as a literary work's author or title, scholarship in composition studies must be classified by terminology that is often less fixed. Scott provides the example of someone researching how writers begin writing; the terms "pre-writing," "invention" and "planning" have all been used to describe this stage of the writing process, yet conducting searches of these words would yield different results. Retrospective searches in composition studies can be difficult, writes Scott, because "even where older research had addressed similar or overlapping questions, the old indexes don't use the expected new words, and a kind of bibliographical amnesia sets in" ("Bibliographical Problems" 169). In addition, Scott writes, what makes the retrieval of relevant sources by subject terms further challenging is that "compositionists tend to talk about more than one topic in an article, and to raise issues that cut across simple subject-categorization" ("Bibliographical Resources" 83).

Still another bibliographic difficulty Scott discusses is that of field demarcation. Scholarship in composition studies is often interdisciplinary, drawing on fields such as education, linguistics, speech communication, cognitive psychology, philosophy, and literary theory. This broad scope of potential inquiry makes it difficult for compilers of bibliographic resources in composition to determine which sources to include and which to exclude when indexing scholarship. Such ill-defined parameters for the discipline also leave researchers uncertain about how fully a subject has been searched when using the bibliographic resources in composition studies. As recently as 2006, librarian Daniel Coffey confirmed the interdisciplinary nature of composition scholarship when he analyzed the citations in a representative sample of the discipline's core monographs and journals. Coffey concluded that "part of what makes composition scholars unique is that their research is not completely encapsulated within the disciplinary realm of the humanities" (162). Perhaps even more than students in traditional humanities disciplines, then, students of composition studies would benefit from a longstanding, comprehensive, user-friendly bibliography.

Unfortunately, the development of a thorough bibliography in composition studies is instead more recent and troubled. Patrick Scott, Paul Bryant, and Richard Haswell have all published historical accounts of the development of bibliographic resources for composition studies, and they all fault the discipline's professional organizations for not developing a comprehensive annual bibliography for the discipline sooner. Scott writes that the sheer multitude of professional organizations in composition studies created a professional segmentation, hindering the commitment of a single organization to devote the money, staff, and resources to a large-scale bibliographic endeavor ("Bibliographical Problems" 172–173). Scott describes this lack of initiative on the part of professional organizations as "embarrassing" ("Bibliographical Resources" 82); Bryant's criticism is equally unforgiving: "That neither the CCCC nor the NCTE saw fit by the mid-1980s to devote some of their considerable publication resources to such a clearly needed, basic professional tool as a comprehensive annual research bibliography when, during that same period, they found it possible to provide significant support to various political and social agendas is regrettable" ("No Longer" 144).

Although helpful volumes were available that offered an introduction to composition scholarship, these also had extensive shortcomings, as Scott explains:

> [I]n addition to being dated, discursive and orientatory guides pose other problems: nearly all the existing guides are avowedly selective in their coverage, most of them are silent about the kinds of searching from which they were compiled, they are often biased one way or another in their selection of material, and most fundamental of all, there are disturbing gaps in the chronological coverage they provide. ("Bibliographical Problems" 167).

What Scott claimed that composition studies still lacked and sorely needed in 1986 when he wrote the above passage was "on-going, systematic, non-judgmental coverage of activity in the field" (167).

This need began to be filled the following year, although it was more than a decade before an annual bibliography in composition studies had a permanent home. In 1987 and 1988, Erika Lindemann edited the *Longman Bibliography of Composition and Rhetoric*, which provided citations and annotations of scholarship in the discipline that was published in 1984–1986. When Longman discontinued this series after publishing just two volumes, the CCCC contracted with Southern Illinois University Press to continue the annual bibliography under the title the *CCCC Bibliography of Composition and Rhetoric*. The nine volumes that followed provide citations and annotations of scholarship in composition studies that was published in 1987–1995. These annual volumes then ceased because the CCCC began plans to join its annual bibliography with the one compiled by the Modern Language Association (MLA); however, Todd Taylor later combined all eleven volumes from both prior publishers and updated them through 1999 into an online, searchable, open access database. Scholarship published after 1999 that would have been included in this annual bibliography, had it been continued, is instead indexed in the *MLA International Bibliography*.

Whereas composition studies once lacked adequate bibliographic resources, such resources for the discipline are now plentiful. In addition to the continuation of the discipline's annual bibliography in the *MLA International Bibliography*, students and professionals can also use CompPile, JSTOR, ERIC, WorldCat and other valuable resources to conduct bibliographic research in composition studies. Because all of these resources differ in how they operate and what they offer, now more than ever, students entering the discipline need bibliographic instruction to gain skill in using these varied resources astutely.

It may be tempting to become comfortable with only one or two bibliographic resources and to assume they will produce adequate results, but Scott warns against this practice, arguing that "in composition, as in other reference fields, we are often channeled by our favorite bibliography's taxonomy and coverage base into one particular research tradition or one phase of a continuing debate, while being cut off from other traditions or phases, and we need, here as in other disciplines, to come to terms with this channeling effect" ("Bibliographical Problems" 176). Elsewhere, Scott reiterates this advice: "For most purposes, it is better to use multiple bibliographical sources rather than relying on a single favorite source—not just because a favorite source might exclude relevant items (different bibliographies have different methodological leanings, for instance), but because in any particular source all the relevant items may not be sorted or indexed under the heading(s) the researcher is using" ("Bibliographical Resources" 88). An important objective of this text, then, is to make you confident about your ability to enhance your search results by using multiple bibliographic resources.

In addition, in keeping with the recommendations of the Association of College & Research Libraries (ACRL) previously discussed, the bibliographic instruction you will learn in this text extends beyond just explaining the tools available to addressing the research process itself. The importance of this approach, as articulated by Scott, is worth quoting at length:

> Practical advice about composition bibliography must therefore be concerned with attitudes and search-strategies, not just with the bibliographies themselves. Often, for instance, when quite sophisticated composition graduate students turn to a bibliographical search, they revert to the worst kind of old-style high-school-research-paper thinking and assume that, given the right subject-heading and the right bibliography, they ought to find readymade *the* list of all necessary material. This could only be true if the research project was a first-level search on a very stable aspect of the discipline. As compositionists should know, research-writing (and therefore research) is not simply about assembling readymade information, but about changing the ways a topic can be looked at and about making new cross-connections between material. ("Bibliographical Resources" 87)

Scott continues by cautioning researchers against relying on "the bibliographer's prepackaged selections" ("Bibliographical Resources" 87) and explains that "specialized bibliographies [. . .] are best used for preliminary orientation to a topic, or for refreshing our sense of the range of material, rather than as a substitute or short-cut for our own systematic library search early in a major project" ("Bibliographical Resources" 79).

What this text will teach you is the processes used by experienced researchers in the discipline, what Scott describes as "search-strategies that maximize [your] own active choosing role" ("Bibliographical Resources" 87). Such strategies are not self-evident in composition studies, making the bibliographic instruction provided in this text necessary. I contend, though, as does Scott, that what makes composition studies bibliographically challenging is what also makes it bibliographically interesting ("Bibliographical Resources" 90–91).

In 1994, Paul Bryant wrote that because bibliographic resources in composition studies now exist, the discipline no longer needs to function as if we face "a brand new world every morning." Yet the bibliographic needs of the discipline are still pressing:

> Perhaps most important, and still much neglected, is the education of graduate students soon to be entering the profession. Use of the ample bibliographic resources in literary studies has been a staple of graduate education in English for generations, but similar instruction in composition and rhetoric is still seldom found, even in some of our most progressive research institutions. This, perhaps, is the next major project for those who would make the study of composition and rhetoric a fully developed academic discipline. We have the tools. Now let us make sure that the next generation of composition teachers and scholars are adequately prepared to use them. ("No Longer" 150)

As I write this chapter fifteen years later, the need for bibliographic instruction in composition studies is still largely unmet. With this book, I hope to fill this need.

Suggestions for Using This Book

The first half of this book provides an introduction to composition studies as a field. More specifically, chapter two explains the modes of inquiry that people in the field use to construct disciplinary knowledge, and chapter three explains the ways in which knowledge in composition studies is disseminated to others in the field. Both of these chapters provide a useful context for helping you to locate work done in composition studies and assess the significance of any source for your own research project as well as its significance to the field. The remaining chapters of this book guide you through your own research process. While reading chapter four, you will make preliminary decisions about your own bibliographic search techniques and criteria. Chapter five will then introduce you to databases and bibliographies that are especially useful to composition studies, and chapter six will guide you through the research and writing process to produce an annotated bibliography and literature review. Even if you are most interested in the discipline-specific databases and guidance for bibliographic assignments that is offered in the final chapters, I recommend that you read this book in sequence and in its entirety because the early chapters will give you knowledge about the field that will help you to make wiser decisions about your research strategies and the individual sources you find. Ultimately, though, you will gain the most from this book if you don't simply read it; you should instead identify a bibliographic project that you can undertake as you read, which will allow you to practice the research strategies and become more adept at using the bibliographic resources discussed in this book.

Perhaps you are encountering this book as a text for a course in which you are enrolled. If so, it is likely that your professor will assign one or more written projects that require you to locate, read, and synthesize prior knowledge in composition studies about a particular topic; the guidance offered in this text can help you to complete those assignments. Or, you may be consulting this book independently of a course, perhaps to hone your research skills in the discipline before beginning an extensive endeavor like writing a thesis or dissertation. Whatever your situation, it can be helpful to identify an issue in composition studies that you'd like to research as you read the remaining chapters of this book.

Take the first step now by formulating a question you would like to research. By using a question to guide your research, rather than just a topic, you will be better able to judge which sources are useful to your research. For example, the research topic "online writing instruction" offers less direction than the research question "What are the best practices in online writing instruction?" or the question "How does online instruction impact students' improvement in writing skills?" Your question should be open-ended, not a question that can be answered with simply a "yes" or "no." Consider writing a group of related questions that you can use to initiate your research, and then after you read some of the sources that these questions help you to find, you can then revise your inquiry, narrowing it to a core question that has not yet been fully resolved by knowledge-makers in the discipline.

If you have difficulty identifying an initial question to research, consider your prior exposure to composition studies. When you think of scholarship you have already read in the discipline, what topics have interested you most? Why? Also, what from your reading have you found most confusing? What could be accomplished by conducting bibliographic research to resolve this confusion? Your experiences as a writer, a writing student, a writing tutor, and/or a writing teacher can serve as additional prompts for research questions. When you have had these experiences, what has puzzled you about the practice, theory, or teaching of writing? If you have thus far had limited exposure to the discipline of composition studies, you may also want to read an introduction to the discipline, which can help you to identify what issues define the discipline. One such introduction is Janice Lauer's essay "Rhetoric and Composition," included in the book *English Studies: An Introduction to the Discipline(s);* the full citation is included in the bibliography at the end of this chapter.

Once you have written your research question(s), write a paragraph that explains why you are interested in this inquiry, then seek feedback on your question(s) and explanatory paragraph from your professor, classmates, and others you may know in composition studies. Although you should then refine your question(s) based on the responses you receive, be aware that once you identify relevant sources and read more about what is already known and what remains to be known about your topic, you will likely need to revise your question(s) again. In other words, just as bibliographic research is a recursive process, so too even the identification of a research topic and question is often recursive, requiring revision throughout your research process.

Some Cautions about This Book

Now that we have examined the need for student-centered introductions to composition studies, for bibliographic instruction in the academy, and for bibliographic instruction specifically in composition studies, and you have identified a research interest to investigate as you read the remainder of this book, I want to conclude this chapter with some cautions about your use of this book, as it is only fair to forewarn you about what this text cannot do.

As should be obvious, this text can't prepare you for what's not available at the time this book is being written. Edward Corbett, a founding member of the profession, has written that "Nothing—not even last year's hemline—dates as quickly as a published bibliography" (qtd. in Scott, "Bibliographical Problems" 167). Fortunately, bibliographic resources do not date as rapidly as do bibliographies themselves, but they too change. For example, when I began writing this book, in only a matter of months several changes took place that required me to make revisions before this book even went to press: the American Psychological Association (APA) issued a new edition of its publication manual; the CompPile and JSTOR databases both got new interfaces, which in turn changed several of their features; several databases added key journals to those they regularly index; and some journals added to their websites the capacity to search the journal's archives. By the time this book appears in print, additional changes affecting bibliographical endeavors in composition studies will undoubtedly have occurred. Much larger changes, such as the increased availability of scholarship through digital formats and open access publishing, are also on the horizon. You will therefore need to update your knowledge of bibliographic resources as the discipline changes in years beyond the publication of this book. However, because this book explains not just bibliographic resources in their current form but also bibliographic strategies, this book will teach you the skills you will need to independently update your knowledge of bibliographic tools.

You should also recognize that while this book will help you to identify scholarship in composition studies relevant to your research interests, finding sources is not the same as understanding and using them well. As librarian Barbara Fister explains, "students must not only be able to find information but to present ideas, shape them to appeal to a particular audience, and support them with convincing evidence. Information must not only be retrieved and evaluated, it must be put to use rhetorically—i.e., used to construct a text" ("Teaching" 212). While bibliographic resources and strategies are the beginning of your own scholarly work in composition studies, they are not all you need to know to participate well in the scholarly conversation. Additional courses in composition studies, as well as your independent reading of scholarship in the discipline, will help you in this regard.

Finally, there are additional issues related to joining the scholarly conversation in composition studies that this book does not discuss. Much has been written about how an author's gender and contractual obligations affect his or her scholarly work in composition studies. There are also published discussions about the appropriate voice for scholarly writing, about experimenting with new forms of publication, and even about the relative merits of teaching and publishing. These are all nuances of the conversation about composition studies scholarship that are beyond the immediate purpose of this book; if these issues interest you, you can learn more about them once you have used this book to enter the composition studies parlor, where these and many other discussions take place.

I urge you, then, to not think of this book as an encyclopedia of all you may ever need to know about scholarship in composition studies. I write it instead as a navigation guide for first-time travelers entering the discipline. If you follow its guidance, you will arrive at your destination—the parlor of composition studies—via the shortest, fastest route, with fewer wrong turns than you'd be likely to make without such a guide. I also hope to direct your journey so that you won't be already exhausted and disoriented upon your arrival but can instead arrive refreshed, ready to listen and learn from the conversation taking place.

Let's begin.

Works Cited

Anderson, Virginia, and Susan Romano, eds. *Culture Shock and the Practice of Profession: Training the Next Wave in Rhetoric & Composition.* Cresskill, NJ: Hampton Press, 2006.

Association of College & Research Libraries. "Information Literacy Competency Standards for Higher Education." January 2000. American Library Association. 19 November 2007 <http://www.ala.org/ala/acrl/acrlstandards/informationliteracycompetency.cfm>

—. "Model Statement of Objectives for Academic Bibliographic Instruction." May 1987. American Library Association. 19 November 2007 <http://www.ala.org/cfapps/archive.cfm?path=acrl/guides/msobi.html>.

—. "Objectives for Information Literacy Instruction: A Model Statement for Academic Librarians." January 2001. American Library Association. 19 November 2007 <http://www.ala.org/ala/acrl/acrlstandards/objectivesinformation.cfm>.

Breivik, Patricia Senn. Foreword. *Higher Education in the Internet Age: Libraries Creating a Strategic Edge.* Patricia Senn Breivik and E. Gordon Gee. Westport, CT: American Council of Education, Praeger Series on Higher Education, 2006. xi-xiv.

Brown, Stuart C., Rebecca Jackson, and Theresa Enos. "The Arrival of Rhetoric in the Twenty-First Century: The 1999 Survey of Doctoral Programs in Rhetoric." *Rhetoric Review* 18 (2000): 233–374.

Brown, Stuart C., Paul R. Meyer, and Theresa Enos. "Doctoral Programs in Rhetoric and Composition: A Catalog of the Profession." *Rhetoric Review* 12 (1994): 240–389.

Brown, Stuart C., Monica F. Torres, Theresa Enos, and Erik Juergensmeyer. "Mapping a Landscape: The 2004 Survey of MA Programs in Rhetoric and Composition Studies." *Rhetoric Review* 24 (2005): 5–12.

Bryant, Paul T. "A Brand New World Every Morning." *College Composition and Communication* 25 (1974): 30–33.

—. "No Longer a Brand New World: The Development of Bibliographic Resources in Composition." *Composition in Context: Essays in Honor of Donald C. Stewart.* Ed. W. Ross Winterowd and Vincent Gillespie. Carbondale: Southern Illinois UP, 1994. 139–51.

Burke, Kenneth. *The Philosophy of Literary Form: Studies in Symbolic Action.* 1941. 3rd edition, revised. Berkeley: U of California P, 1973.

Chapman, David W., and Gary Tate. "A Survey of Doctoral Programs in Rhetoric and Composition." *Rhetoric Review* 5 (1987): 124–85.

Coffey, Daniel P. "A Discipline's Composition: A Citation Analysis of Composition Studies." *The Journal of Academic Librarianship* 32 (2006): 155–65.

Connors, Robert J. "Composition History and Disciplinarity." *History, Reflection, and Narrative: The Professionalization of Composition, 1963–1983.* Ed. Mary Rosner, Beth Boehm, and Debra Journet. Stamford, CT: Ablex, 1999. 3–21.

Curzon, Susan Carol. "Developing Faculty-Librarian Partnerships in Information Literacy." *Integrating Information Literacy into the Higher Education Curriculum: Practical Models for Transformation.* Ed. Ilene F. Rockman. San Francisco, CA: Jossey-Bass, 2004. 29–46.

Fister, Barbara. "Common Ground: The Composition/Bibliographic Instruction Connection." *Academic Libraries: Achieving Excellence in Higher Education. Proceedings of the Sixth National Conference of the Association of College and Research Libraries.* Ed. Thomas Kirk. Chicago: Association of College and Research Libraries, 1992. 154–58.

—. "Teaching the Rhetorical Dimensions of Research." *Research Strategies* 11 (1993): 211–19.

Fontaine, Sheryl I., and Susan M. Hunter. "Inviting Students into Composition Studies with a New Instructional Genre." *Culture Shock and the Practice of Profession: Training the New Wave in Rhetoric and Composition.* Ed. Virginia Anderson and Susan Romano. Cresskill, NJ: Hampton, 2006. 197–213.

Hardesty, Larry. "Faculty Culture and Bibliographic Instruction: An Exploratory Analysis." *Library Trends* 44 (1995): 339–67.

Haswell, Richard H. "NCTE/CCCC's Recent War on Scholarship." *Written Communication* 22 (2005): 198–223.

Kohl, David F., and Lizabeth A. Wilson. "Effectiveness of Course-Integrated Bibliographic Instruction in Improving Coursework." *Reference Quarterly* 26 (1986): 206–11.

Lauer, Janice M. "Graduate Students as Active Members of the Profession: Some Questions for Mentoring." *Publishing in Rhetoric and Composition.* Ed. Gary A. Olson and Todd W. Taylor. Albany: SUNY P, 1997. 229–35.

—. "Rhetoric and Composition." *English Studies: An Introduction to the Discipline(s).* Ed. Bruce McComiskey. Urbana, IL: NCTE, 2006. 106–52.

Olson, Gary A. "Publishing Scholarship in Rhetoric and Composition: Joining the Conversation." *Publishing in Rhetoric and Composition.* Ed. Gary A. Olson and Todd W. Taylor. Albany: SUNY P, 1997. 19–33.

Peirce, Karen P., and Theresa Jarnagin Enos. "How Seriously Are We Taking Professionalization? A Report on Graduate Curricula in Rhetoric and Composition." *Rhetoric Review* 25 (2006): 204–10.

Phelps, Louise Wetherbee. "Writing the New Rhetoric of Scholarship." *Defining the New Rhetorics.* Sage Series in Written Communication Volume 7. Ed. Theresa Enos and Stuart C. Brown. Newbury Park, CA: Sage, 1993. 55–78.

Rockman, Ilene F. "Introduction: The Importance of Information Literacy." *Integrating Information Literacy into the Higher Education Curriculum: Practical Models for Transformation.* Ed. Ilene F. Rockman. San Francisco: Jossey-Bass, 2004. 1–28.

Scott, Patrick. "Bibliographical Problems in Research on Composition." *College Composition and Communication* 37 (1986): 167–77.

—. "Bibliographic Resources and Problems." *An Introduction to Composition Studies.* Ed. Erika Lindemann and Gary Tate. New York: Oxford UP, 1991. 72–93.

For Further Reading

Berkenkotter, Carol, Thomas N. Huckin, and John Ackerman. "Conventions, Conversation, and the Writer: Case Study of a Student in a Rhetoric Ph.D. Program." *Research in the Teaching of English* 22 (1988): 9–44.

Borgman, Christine L. *Scholarship in the Digital Age: Information, Infrastructure and the Internet.* Cambridge, MA: MIT Press, 2007.

Breivik, Patricia Senn, and E. Gordon Gee. *Higher Education in the Internet Age: Libraries Creating a Strategic Edge.* Westport, CT: American Council of Education, Praeger Series on Higher Education, 2006.

Fister, Barbara. "Connected Communities: Encouraging Dialogue Between Composition and Bibliographic Instruction." *Writing-Across-the-Curriculum and the Academic Library: A Guide for Librarians, Instructors, and Writing Program Directors.* Ed. Jean Sheridan. Westport, CT: Greenwood, 1995. 33–51.

Lauer, Janice M., and Andrea Lunsford. "The Place of Rhetoric and Composition Studies in Doctoral Programs." *The Future of Doctoral Studies in English.* Ed. Andrea Lunsford, Helene Moglen, and James Slevin. New York: MLA, 1989. 106–10.

Lindemann, Erika. "Early Bibliographic Work in Composition Studies." *Profession.* New York: Modern Language Association, 2002. 151–57.

Lindemann, Erika, and Gary Tate, eds. *An Introduction to Composition Studies.* New York: Oxford UP, 1991.

Lunsford, Andrea, Helene Moglen, and James F. Slevin. *The Future of Doctoral Studies in English.* New York: MLA, 1989.

North, Stephen M., Barbara A. Chepaitis, David Coogan, Lale Davidgon, Ron MacLean, Cindy L. Parrish, Jonathan Post, and Beth Weatherby. *Refiguring the Ph.D. in English Studies: Writing, Doctoral Education, and the Fusion-Based Curriculum.* Urbana, IL: NCTE, 2000.

Nystand, Martin, Stuart Greene, and Jeffrey Wiemelt. "Where Did Composition Studies Come From? An Intellectual History." *Written Communication* 10 (1993): 267–33.

Raspa, Dick, and Dane Ward, eds. *The Collaborative Imperative: Librarians and Faculty Working Together in the Information Universe.* Chicago: American Library Association, 2000.

Rockman, Ilene F., ed. *Integrating Information Literacy into the Higher Education Curriculum: Practical Models for Transformation.* San Francisco: Jossey-Bass, 2004.

Scott, Patrick, and Bruce Castner. "Reference Sources for Composition Research: A Practical Survey." *College English* 45 (1983): 756–68.

Sheridan, Jean. "What Bibliographic Instruction Librarians Can Learn from Writing-Across-the-Curriculum Instructors." *Writing-Across-the-Curriculum and the Academic Library: A Guide for Librarians, Instructors, and Writing Program Directors.* Ed. Jean Sheridan. Westport, CT: Greenwood, 1995. 113–19.

2 Voices in the Parlor: The Construction of Knowledge in Composition Studies

The first chapter of this book opened with an analogy that compared scholarship in an academic discipline to an ongoing conversation taking place in a parlor. Although a parlor seems a more antiquated reference now than it likely did when Kenneth Burke published this analogy in 1941, the notion of a conversation taking place within a designated space is still vital to an understanding of disciplinary knowledge. A conversation taking place in a parlor implies that those inside the room understand and practice conversation differently than do those who are outside the room. One defining element of the conversation in each academic discipline's parlor is how the discipline creates new knowledge, specifically, which modes of inquiry the discipline values and what the discipline accepts as convincing evidence.

The purpose of this chapter is to introduce you to how knowledge is constructed in composition studies. As a student and newcomer to composition studies, you need to learn about the discipline's methods of creating and testing knowledge so that as you engage in bibliographic research, you can better assess the significance of each source you find, each voice you encounter in the conversation. Learning more about how knowledge is constructed in composition studies can also prepare you to search for the full spectrum of voices that contribute to knowledge about your research interest so that your bibliographic research is as comprehensive as possible.

The most well-known account of how knowledge is formed in composition studies is the book *The Making of Knowledge in Composition: Portrait of an Emerging Field*, written by Stephen North. In this book, North proposes a taxonomy of knowledge in composition studies based on what he calls its "modes of inquiry—the whole series of steps an inquirer follows in making a contribution to a field of knowledge" (1). North argues that the modes of inquiry used in composition studies comprise three major "methodological communities" (1): scholars, researchers, and practitioners. Though *The Making of Knowledge in Composition* was published in 1987, it remains a core text in many graduate composition studies programs because it continues to serve as a helpful introduction to how knowledge is constructed in the discipline. Using the framework provided by North's book, let us now examine further each of these core modes of inquiry in composition studies: scholarship, empirical research, and practice. The following sections provide a definition, some examples, and advice for locating each.

SCHOLARSHIP

Definition of Scholarship

The most traditional mode of knowledge in composition studies is scholarship. North defines scholarship as a mode of inquiry that is text-based and that relies on dialectic, which he defines as "the seeking of knowledge via the deliberate confrontation of opposing points of view" (60). North identifies three major types of knowledge-makers who produce scholarship in composition studies: historians, philosophers, and critics. He describes them more fully as "those who seek knowledge about how rhetoric has been understood and practiced in the past [the historians]; or who try to get at the theoretical underpinning of rhetorical activity [the philosophers]; or whose approach to textual interpretation has a rhetorical basis [the critics]" (64). Although he says that many of the people he designates as scholars would self-identify as rhetoricians, he does not use that term in his own taxonomy of knowledge-makers in the discipline.

Examples of Scholarship

Examples of scholarship can be found for any issue in composition studies; here, the topic of writing across the curriculum (often identified by the acronym WAC) will be used to provide some concrete examples of the how scholarship contributes to knowledge in composition studies. One example of historical scholarship about writing across the curriculum is "The History of the WAC Movement," an early chapter in Bazerman et al.'s *Reference Guide to Writing Across the Curriculum* (2005). This chapter provides a concise history that describes the origins of writing instruction in colleges and universities in the late nineteenth century, cites some initial arguments for writing across the curriculum that emerged in the 1930s, and then traces how political and social changes that impacted college enrollments in later decades, along with educational reform movements in Britain in the 1960s and 1970s, led to the recognition of a need to teach writing skills in multiple disciplines. The chapter then identifies when formal writing-across-the-curriculum programs were institutionalized and concludes by discussing the initiation of journals, conferences, and web resources that provided further support for the development of WAC knowledge and practice.

McLeod and Soven's book *Composing a Community: A History of Writing Across the Curriculum* (2006) is also a history of WAC, but as a collection of twelve essays by different authors, it is both more selective and more detailed in its historical approach. Here, readers will find histories of particular emphases in WAC, such as Barbara Walvoord's essay "Gender and Discipline in Two Early WAC Communities: Lessons for Today," as well as a numerous essays that discuss the history of the WAC program at particular institutions: George Mason University, the California State University system, the University of Chicago, and Michigan Tech, to name a few. As Bazerman et al.'s chapter and McLeod and Soven's book illustrate, histories in composition studies contribute to disciplinary knowledge by identifying the factors that have influenced some aspect of the field. In turn, that understanding of historical influences can provide insight into how the topic is currently configured in the discipline; also, histories often yield cautionary advice or recommendations for future developments in the discipline.

In addition to histories, another type of scholarship, according to North, is philosophy, what we would now more commonly term as theory; North himself described philosophers in composition studies as those who "try to get at the theoretical underpinning of rhetorical activity" (64). In composition studies, theory is often the form of knowledge-building that most depends on dialectic, which again, North defines as "the seeking of knowledge via the deliberate confrontation of opposing points of view" (60). At times, theory can be contentious. Consider, for example, McLeod's and Maimon's article

"Clearing the Air: WAC Myths and Realities," published in *College English* in 2000. The authors begin by identifying four ways in which they believe other scholars have mischaracterized the history, definition, and effectiveness of WAC. After discussing why others' characterizations of WAC are "myths," McLeod and Maimon then posit theories that they contend more accurately represent the relationship between WAC and writing to learn and writing in the disciplines, as well as the intertwined elements of WAC programs.

Often, scholarship in composition studies that is theoretical is developed because the author wants to expand on—rather than to correct—earlier scholarship. An example of such scholarship is Samuels' article "Re-Inventing the Modern University with WAC: Postmodern Composition as Cultural and Intellectual History" (2004). Here, Samuels contrasts the traits of modernism and postmodernism, then theorizes that WAC is perfectly suited for the postmodern university because its focus on disciplinary discourse challenges students to examine the epistemologies of different disciplines. Thus, this article furthers knowledge about WAC by merging it with postmodern theory and educational philosophy; often, scholars in composition studies similarly apply theories that originated in other disciplines to issues in composition studies in ways that expand knowledge in our discipline.

The final form of scholarship identified by North is criticism, undertaken by those "whose approach to textual interpretation has a rhetorical basis" (64). One example of textual criticism in composition studies, specifically WAC, is Ochsner and Fowler's article "Playing Devil's Advocate: Evaluating the Literature of the WAC/WID Movement," published in *Review of Educational Research* in 2004. For this article, Ochsner and Fowler analyzed eighty publications about writing across the curriculum (WAC) and writing in the disciplines (WID). Their analysis of these texts led the authors to identify several specific weaknesses in published scholarship and studies about WAC: these texts often don't clearly distinguish between writing to learn and learning to write; texts about WAC privilege writing as the primary mode of learning and do not adequately acknowledge other modes of learning, such as speaking, listening, and reading; the effectiveness of WAC is too often based on self-reports of faculty and students rather than more independent measures of student learning; the financial costs of WAC programs—including faculty development, program administration, program assessment, and smaller class sizes—are regularly underestimated in WAC literature; and WAC literature often does not recognize the training required for faculty to teach writing well. What distinguishes scholarship as criticism is not that it is negative in its emphasis, but rather that it is scholarship that contributes to knowledge in composition studies by analyzing the strengths and weaknesses of other scholarly texts.

Advice for Locating Scholarship

Most of the bibliographic work you will do in composition studies will entail locating and synthesizing scholarship. As you have undoubtedly learned during your undergraduate education, most scholarship is not readily available on the internet, especially through general search engines like Google and Yahoo. Whereas anything can be posted on the web, regardless of its accuracy, scholarly writing must meet more rigorous standards that ensure its credibility. One of the distinguishing characteristics of scholarly writing is that it is written by authors who are experts in the discipline and who use discipline-specific terminology when discussing ideas with readers who are also knowledgeable about the discipline; also, scholarly writing includes citations to other sources that the writer has consulted in developing the text. In addition, most scholarly manuscripts are subjected to peer review prior to being accepted for publication. Peer review means that others in the discipline who are knowledgeable about the topic being discussed read the manuscript, decide whether it's worthy of publication, and offer suggestions to improve it prior to its publication. Scholarly writing is usually only accepted for publication if it addresses issues that are of interest to the profession, contains accurate, well-supported arguments, and makes an original contribution to the knowledge of the discipline. Published scholarship that has undergone peer review is generally considered credible and worthy of the attention of others in the discipline, who then read, discuss, and incorporate the knowledge produced by the text into their own work, thus continuing the disciplinary conversation.

Scholarship is published primarily as books, essays in edited collections, and articles in scholarly journals. To locate scholarship, you must use resources such as library catalogues and databases; the major databases and bibliographic resources for finding scholarship in composition studies will be discussed extensively in chapter five of this book.

For Writing and Discussion

1. Consider the issue in composition studies that you want to research as you read this book. How do you expect that the scholarship you locate will help you to better understand this issue?

2. North identifies three types of scholarship: history, philosophy or theory, and textual criticism. When doing bibliographic research in composition studies, how important is it that you find sources that represent all three kinds of scholarship? How might each of these types of scholarship contribute uniquely to your understanding of an issue in composition studies?

EMPIRICAL RESEARCH

Definition of Empirical Research

When North identifies another methodological community within the discipline as "researchers," he is referring to those who conduct empirical research studies to build knowledge in composition studies. Because an empirical researcher collects data directly from participants in a study, empirical research is also known as primary research; in contrast, scholarship is sometimes called secondary research because it relies on knowledge gained through other texts, i.e., knowledge a writer gains secondhand. An empirical researcher builds knowledge by collecting and analyzing data, then publishing these results in article-length or book-length research reports.

Though North identified several methods of empirical research in his book, he admitted that his was only a partial list of the methods being used by researchers in composition studies. More complete explanations of empirical research methods being used in composition studies were published in the years following North's book, in texts such as Lauer and Asher's *Composition Research: Empirical Designs* (1988), MacNealy's *Strategies for Empirical Research in Writing* (1999), and Blakeslee and Fleischer's *Becoming a Writing Researcher* (2007).

Though there are many empirical research designs used in composition studies, most can be classified as being either qualitative or quantitative. Qualitative research designs study either a small number of participants (a case study) or a larger number of participants within their environment (an ethnography), and have as their goal the identification of specific variables that describe the participants' natural behavior concerning an issue related to composition studies. The data in qualitative research are typically descriptive observations; the researcher then uses those observations to state more specific conclusions or findings and to suggest implications for the discipline on the basis of those findings. Two well-known examples of qualitative studies in composition studies are Janet Emig's case study *The Composing Processes of Twelfth Graders* and Shirley Brice Heath's ethnography *Ways with Words*.

Quantitative research differs from qualitative research in that it typically contrasts a treatment and a control group to test the validity of a hypothesis. As a simple example, a teacher may teach one classroom of students as she typically does, while she teaches a different classroom of students using an experimental pedagogy, the "treatment" that she is testing. While carefully controlling for possible interferences to the study, known as threats to validity, the researcher collects data from both groups of students to determine whether the new pedagogy has a significant effect on students' performance. Findings in quantitative studies are typically reported numerically (rather than descriptively, as in qualitative studies) and often depend on rigorous statistical analyses. Two journals known for publishing reports of quantitative research in composition studies are *Research in the Teaching of English* and *Written Communication*. Yet another form of quantitative research is a meta-analysis, which is a study that selects from many prior quantitative studies according to carefully chosen criteria and then statistically consolidates their findings. The most well-known meta-analysis in composition studies is George Hillocks' *Research on Written Composition*.

Examples of Empirical Research

For examples of how empirical research contributes to knowledge in composition studies, let us return to the topic of writing across the curriculum. WAC has been the subject of both qualitative and quantitative empirical research studies, and the published results of these studies extend the knowledge about WAC beyond what can be learned from scholarship. Much of the empirical research about WAC is qualitative. Beaufort's article "Developmental Gains of a History Major: A Case for Building a Theory of Disciplinary Writing Expertise" (2004) is just one example of several case studies that have been undertaken to identify how an individual student learned the complexities of writing in a particular discipline. Other qualitative studies about WAC have focused not on student learning but on faculty development, such as Walvoord et al.'s *In the Long Run: A Study of Faculty in Three Writing-Across-the-Curriculum Programs* (1997), which examines the impact of WAC on several faculties' teaching philosophies and attitudes, teaching strategies, and career patterns. A characteristic shared by many of the qualitative studies about WAC is that they are longitudinal studies, i.e., studies in which data is collected over multiple years.

Although quantitative research studies about WAC are less common, some are available. One example is Beason's article "Feedback and Revision in Writing Across the Curriculum Classes," published in *Research in the Teaching of English* in 1993. This study did not entail a treatment and control group; instead, a total of twenty students were randomly selected from writing classes in four disciplines, and the first and final drafts of these students' multi-draft writing assignments were analyzed by multiple raters, who coded the feedback students received on their drafts and the revisions that students made. All of the data was then quantified so that precise conclusions could be drawn about the differences in teacher and student feedback on drafts, as well as the relationship between comments and the revisions that students made. Beason also compared the data from this study of feedback and revision in WAC courses to data from other studies about feedback and revision in traditional composition courses.

Beason explains in his article that he chose a quantitative design for his study because of its unique potential to contribute to the discipline's knowledge about WAC, especially in contrast to the many qualitative studies about WAC that were already available:

> Although [prior qualitative WAC studies] are insightful studies, a focused quantitative approach (besides helping create a needed balance in WAC research) allows a researcher to isolate and scrutinize selected phenomena that are affected by many classroom factors but that can still be singled out and examined in and of themselves. Coding such phenomena provides, moreover, a sense of order for complex behaviors and products that seem to be without patterns . . . (406)

He further comments that his study contributes not only to knowledge about WAC but also to knowledge about feedback on writing and revision. Because quantitative studies often analyze data about multiple variables, it is common for a single quantitative study to contribute to the discipline's knowledge about more than one topic.

Another example of a quantitative research about WAC is a meta-analysis. Bangert-Drowns et al. published "The Effects of School-Based Writing-to-Learn Interventions on Academic Achievement: A Meta-Analysis" in *Review of Educational Research* in 2004. These authors quantitatively analyzed the reports of forty-eight previously published research studies about writing-to-learn curricula at a range of grade levels and in a range of disciplines (this latter variable is what makes this meta-analysis relevant to WAC). After consolidating the results of all these studies, using methods appropriate for meta-analyses, the authors concluded that "writing can have a small, positive impact on conventional measures of academic achievement" (29). Other conclusions of this meta-analysis are that the effects are greater if the writing prompts are used for a longer period of time and if the writing prompts require metacognition, but the effects are lessened if these writing curricula are implemented in middle school grades or if the writing assignments are too long. The results of meta-analyses are more noteworthy than the results of a single research study because they help to combine and appropriately weight the findings of many studies, thereby contributing substantially to knowledge in the discipline.

Advice for Locating Empirical Research

When you are conducting bibliographic research, do not dismiss empirical research that has relevance to your topic simply because its methodology and reporting may seem unfamiliar to you. Empirical studies provide valuable knowledge to the discipline, so much so that when Richard Haswell, one of the founders of CompPile (a major database in composition studies), noticed that two of the main professional organizations in composition studies have discouraged the publication of empirical research, he charged those organizations with waging a war on disciplinary knowledge. Haswell argues that the consequences of dismissing empirical research are severe: "when college composition as a whole treats the data-gathering, data-validating, and data-aggregating part of itself as alien, then the whole may be doomed"

(219). Haswell cites others who share his stance, including Stephen Witte, who states, "A field that presumes the efficacy of a particular research methodology, a particular inquiry paradigm, will collapse inward upon itself" (qtd. in Haswell 220). To limit this threat, Haswell has coined the term "RAD research" to refer to research in composition studies that is replicable, aggregable, and data supported; he has also restricted CompPile's use of the search term "data" to refer to "any study that systematically collects and reports facts usable in further study, through whatever research method (interview, ethnography, experimentation, descriptive measurement, case study, etc.)" (Haswell, CompPile Glossary).

When investigating an issue for your bibliographic project, you can use several of the databases that you will learn more about in chapter five—CompPile, WorldCat, ERIC and JSTOR—to search specifically for reports of empirical research. When using the CompPile database, you can locate empirical research by using the search terms for your topic in conjunction with the search terms "RAD research" or "data." To find any book-length research reports published on your topic, conduct an advanced search of the WorldCat database, using the keywords for your topic along with the following Library of Congress subject descriptor: "English language—Composition and Exercises—Research" (it must be typed using two hyphens to represent each dash). Using the ERIC database, you can more easily identify reports of empirical research on your topic if you limit your search to just the two journals that publish the greatest number of empirical research reports about composition studies: *Research in the Teaching of English* and *Written Communication*. Additional journals that publish empirical research reports about topics in education more broadly are indexed in the JSTOR database; the journal *Review of Educational Research,* which published the meta-analysis about WAC discussed as an example here, is one such journal. After you have read chapter five to learn more about these databases, return to the advice offered here if your initial bibliographic searches on an issue yield insufficient empirical research.

For Writing and Discussion

1. Have you had exposure to empirical research methods, perhaps through courses you have taken in other disciplines? If so, how would you describe the value of empirical research as a means of

constructing disciplinary knowledge? If you have not been previously exposed to empirical research methods, what questions do you have about this mode of inquiry based on what you have just read?

2. In his article about how some professional organizations in composition studies have discouraged the publication of empirical research, Richard Haswell depicts these actions as waging a war on disciplinary knowledge. What do you think of Haswell's use of the word "war" in this context? Why do you think that those who are engaged in composition studies may differ in their assessment of the value of empirical research?

3. As explained in this section, two major types of empirical research are qualitative studies and quantitative studies. How might each contribute uniquely to the construction of knowledge in composition studies? In what ways might it be important when conducting bibliographic research in composition studies to look for both qualitative and quantitative studies?

4. Consider the issue in composition studies that you want to research as you read this book. How do you expect that empirical research reports you locate will help you to better understand this issue?

PRACTICE

Definition of Practice

The final way that knowledge is formed in composition studies, according to North, is through the practical experience of teachers, tutors, and writing program administrators. North calls knowledge that is based on practical experience "lore," which he defines as "the accumulated body of traditions, practices, and beliefs in terms of which practitioners understand how writing is done, learned, and taught" (22). North writes that practice doesn't always contribute to disciplinary knowledge; instead, North sets the condition that practice can only deservedly be considered inquiry "whenever it contributes to lore—only when, in short, it produces 'new' knowledge" (33). He estimates that for a college teacher employed full-time, practice may qualify as inquiry "less than ten percent of the time" (34).

For North, one of the distinguishing characteristics of lore is that it is uncritical. This can be deduced from North's delineation of what he calls "three of its most important functional properties" (24): anything can become lore if someone suggests it; there is no method of removing anything from lore, even if it contradicts other lore; lore is practical (24–25). North also discusses lore as ultimately individualistic:

> But whereas in other communities the greatest authority over what constitutes knowledge resides with the community—lies, in effect, with *public* knowledge—here it lies with the individual Practitioner, and *private* knowledge. The communal lore offers options, resources, and perhaps some directional pressure; but the individual, finally, decides what to do and whether (or how) it has worked—decides, in short, what counts as knowledge. (28)

In her essay "Practical Wisdom and the Geography of Knowledge in Composition," Louise Wetherbee Phelps critiques and refines North's concept of practice as knowledge. Phelps argues that practitioners deserve a stronger role as thinkers who contribute to "the knowledge enterprise of composition" than North allows in crediting them only with uncritical, individualist lore. Phelps proposes instead a taxonomy of knowledge in composition that includes scholarship, research, and three distinct types of what she calls practical knowledge: lore, art, and local knowledge. Her definition of lore is consistent with North's use of the term: unreflective, experience-based, and limited in influence to each individual's daily practice.

The other two types of practical knowledge that Phelps delineates—art and local knowledge—differ from lore in that both are reflective and entail critical judgment. Also, both are subject to evaluation and revision by a local community of practitioners. The difference between art and local knowledge is that art is derived from and informs practice—Phelps calls it "reflection-in-action" (876)—whereas local knowledge is inquiry about practice that is temporarily detached from action (877). Together, art and local knowledge, manifested as action and inquiry, build new knowledge about composition studies, particularly for the students, departments, and institutions that those practitioners serve. The model Phelps provides of practice as knowledge-making is that of a community of reflective practitioners, for example, "a teaching community collectively developing and testing a curriculum" (866).

Examples of Practice

Once more, let us return to the topic of writing across the curriculum to consider how practice contributes to knowledge about a topic in composition studies. Occasionally, practical knowledge can be located through a search for books and journal articles; one example of a book that is practical knowledge about WAC is Chris Anson's edited collection *The WAC Casebook: Scenes for Faculty Reflection and Program Development*. Although this book is published by an academic press, it is better classified as practical knowledge than as scholarship because its forty-five brief chapters each provide solely a description of a dilemma, based on WAC practice, that is meant to serve as a prompt for reflection and discussion; no theories, recommendations or solutions are offered.

A significant source of knowledge based on practice is institutional websites. Often, these websites need to be located and examined individually, which is what Dan Metzer did when he visited course websites to collect nearly eight hundred WAC assignments from forty-eight institutions; he used these assignments as the basis for his article "Assignments Across the Curriculum: A Survey of College Writing." Some topics in composition studies may already be organized in a central location online; for example, the WAC Clearinghouse (http://wac.colostate.edu) provides links to many institutions' WAC program sites under its resources tab. An exploration of the WAC Clearinghouse site leads to other helpful lore, such as a very practical question and answer introduction to WAC for teachers (with questions like "How can I avoid getting lousy student papers?" and "Why consider collaborative writing assignments?"). However, even when an internet site is available that serves as a central location for practical knowledge about a particular topic, it is still useful to search the internet for helpful sites that may be more recent or that may offer different perspectives on practice.

Advice for Locating Practice

When you are conducting bibliographic research, you will need to determine the extent to which you should research practical knowledge in the discipline about your research topic. Although occasionally practical knowledge is chronicled in publications that you can locate through traditional catalogues and databases (for example, a journal article, essay, or book that describes a particular curriculum or other practice at a particular university), often you will need to look elsewhere for records of practical knowledge. One source of published practical knowledge is composition textbooks and the instructor's manuals that sometimes accompany them. In some cases, statements of practical knowledge will be available on the websites of professional organizations related to composition studies. Other storehouses for practical knowledge include wikis (such as the CompFAQs wiki that is affiliated with the CompPile database), the websites of writing programs and the professional websites of practitioners in the discipline, and the archives of mailing lists that are related to composition studies. In chapter three of this book, you will learn how to locate these types of online sites. For some historical projects, you may even need to request print archives from an institution or an individual. You can also locate archival materials at the National Archives of Composition and Rhetoric and audio and visual archives at the Rhetoric and Composition Sound Archives; the websites for both are provided in the bibliography at the end of this chapter.

Be aware that written records of practical knowledge will vary widely in their credibility. Unlike published scholarship and research, records of practical knowledge will rarely have been subjected to critical review. Therefore, you should take great care in deciding what is worthy of inclusion in your own project. Be aware that practical knowledge, while often helpful because it is specific and pragmatic, may be perceived as having little relevance for situations beyond its immediate context. Also, the audience for any written records of practical knowledge may vary widely; documents may be written for students, for fellow practitioners, for administrators, or even for an audience whose identity you cannot discern. I do not offer these cautions intending to suggest that accounts of practical knowledge are necessarily inferior to other forms of knowledge in the discipline; rather, my aim is to emphasize that practical knowledge is the only form of knowledge you might cite in your bibliographic research that is not likely to have been peer reviewed. You therefore should be prepared to be especially discerning about the materials themselves as well as their usefulness to your bibliographic project.

For Writing and Discussion

1. Most disciplines do not explicitly acknowledge practice as a means of constructing new knowledge. Discuss your reaction to North's and Phelps's emphasis on practice as a means of building new disciplinary knowledge in composition studies. If you have had an opportunity to engage in professional practice related to composition studies—perhaps as a tutor, a graduate teaching assistant, or a teacher—describe an experience you have had that you think has resulted in new knowledge that might rightfully be called practical knowledge.

2. Consider the issue in composition studies that you want to research as you read this book. How do you expect that sources you locate that describe practical knowledge will help you to better understand this issue?

3. As discussed throughout this chapter, the discipline of composition studies depends on multiple modes of inquiry for the production of new knowledge: scholarship, empirical research, and practice. In what ways might the use of multiple modes of inquiry be an asset to the discipline? In what ways might the use of multiple modes of inquiry be a hindrance to the discipline?

HYBRID KNOWLEDGE

Although the categories above—scholarship, empirical research, and practical knowledge—have been discussed as discrete modes of knowledge in composition studies, it is more accurate to expect that whatever you read in composition studies will *primarily* take one of the above approaches but will likely include the others as well. For example, because composition studies is a discipline greatly concerned with pedagogy, much scholarship will include anecdotes about the particular students, student texts, or classroom situations that provoked the development of a newly proposed theory. Thus, scholarship often emerges from practice, just as scholarship often draws conclusions meant to impact practice. Also, even though empirical research relies on the collection and analysis of data, most research reports begin with a review of prior scholarship in order to contextualize the research, and research reports often conclude with implications for practice.

Therefore, scholarship, empirical research, and practical knowledge are often all present in research reports. Similarly, records of practical knowledge may often call for and allude to scholarship and research when practical knowledge alone seems inadequate for addressing the issues at hand. Thus, although the modes of inquiry in composition studies function differently, in published writings they often merge, intersect, and overlap.

In 1987, North considered the variety of methodological communities in composition studies to be a threat to the discipline. He described the discipline as engaged in "a methodological land rush: a scramble to stake out territory, to claim power over what constitutes knowledge in Composition; and to claim, as well, whatever rewards that power might carry with it" (317). He warned that one condition necessary for composition studies to survive as a discipline was "to find some way to establish an internal, inter-methodological peace [. . .] so that the methodological pluralism that was responsible for creating Composition in the first place can remain its vital core" (369). More than twenty years later, the discipline is thriving, in part because its modes of inquiry are so richly varied and so intertwined. Together, scholarship, research, and practice provide a more multifaceted understanding of the complex issues in the discipline than would be possible with any single mode of inquiry. When conducting bibliographic research, to accurately represent the rich conversation taking place in the composition studies parlor, you should draw on them all.

Works Cited

Anson, Chris M., ed. *The WAC Casebook: Scenes for Faculty Reflection and Program Development*. Oxford: Oxford UP, 2002.

Bangert-Drowns, Robert L., Marlene M. Hurley, and Barbara Wilkinson. "The Effects of School-Based Writing-to-Learn Interventions on Academic Achievement: A Meta-Analysis." *Review of Educational Research* 74 (2004): 29–58.

Bazerman, Charles, Joseph Little, Lisa Bethel, Teri Chavkin, Danielle Fouquette, and Janet Garufis. *Reference Guide to Writing Across the Curriculum*. West Lafayette, IN: Parlor Press, 2005.

Beason, Larry. "Feedback and Revision in Writing Across the Curriculum Classes." *Research in the Teaching of English* 27 (1993): 395–422.

Beaufort, Anne. "Developmental Gains of a History Major: A Case for Build-
    ing a Theory of Disciplinary Writing Expertise." *Research in the Teaching
    of English* 39 (2004): 136–85.

Blakeslee, Ann M., and Cathy Fleischer. *Becoming a Writing Researcher.*
    Mahwah, NJ: Erlbaum, 2007.

Emig, Janet. *The Composing Processes of Twelfth Graders.* NCTE research re-
    port No 13. Urbana, IL: National Council of Teachers of English, 1971.

Haswell, Richard. CompPile Glossary. 18 September 2008 <http://comppile.
    org/glossary/glossary_list.php>.

—. "NCTE/CCCC's Recent War on Scholarship." *Written Communication*
    22 (2005): 198–223.

Heath, Shirley Brice. *Ways with Words: Language, Life, and Work in Commu-
    nities and Classrooms.* Cambridge, England: Cambridge UP, 1983.

Hillocks, George Jr. *Research on Written Composition: New Directions for
    Teaching.* Urbana, IL: ERIC Clearinghouse on Reading and Communi-
    cation Skills, National Institute of Education, 1986.

Lauer, Janice, and J. William Asher. *Composition Research: Empirical Designs.*
    New York: Oxford UP, 1988.

MacNealy, Mary Sue. *Strategies for Empirical Research in Writing.* Boston:
    Allyn and Bacon, 1999.

McLeod, Susan, and Elaine Maimon. "Clearing the Air: WAC Myths and
    Realities." *College English* 62 (2000): 573–83.

McLeod, Susan H., and Margaret Iris Soven, ed. *Composing a Community:
    A History of Writing Across the Curriculum.* West Lafayette, IN: Parlor
    Press, 2006.

Metzer, Dan. "Assignments Across the Curriculum: A Survey of College
    Writing." *Language and Learning Across the Disciplines* 6 (2003). 13 March
    2009 <http://wac.colostate.edu/llad/v6n1/melzer.pdf>.

National Archives of Composition and Rhetoric. September 4, 2008. Uni-
    versity of Rhode Island. 20 September 2008 <http://www.uri.edu/artsci/
    writing/projects/archives.shtml>.

North, Stephen M. *The Making of Knowledge in Composition: Portrait of an
    Emerging Field.* Portsmouth, NH: Boynton/Cook, Heinemann, 1987.

Ochsner, Robert, and Judy Fowler. "Playing Devil's Advocate: Evaluating the
    Literature of the WAC/WID Movement." *Review of Educational Research*
    74 (2004): 117–40.

Phelps, Louise Wetherbee. "Practical Wisdom and the Geography of Knowl-
    edge in Composition." *College English* 53 (1991): 863–85.

Rhetoric and Composition Sound Archives. January 26, 2007. Texas Chris-
    tian University. 20 September 2008 <http://www.rcsa.tcu.edu/>.

Samuels, Robert. "Re-Inventing the Modern University with WAC:
    Postmodern Composition as Cultural and Intellectual History." *Across*

the Disciplines 1 (2004). 13 March 2009 <http://wac.colostate.edu/atd/articles/samuels2004.cfm>.

Walvoord, Barbara E., Linda Lawrence Hunt, H. Fil Dowling Jr., and Joan D. McMahon. *In the Long Run: A Study of Faculty in Three Writing-Across-the-Curriculum Programs.* Urbana, IL: NCTE, 1997. WAC Clearinghouse. 13 March 2009 <http://wac.colostate.edu>.

FOR FURTHER READING

Dobrin, Sidney. *Constructing Knowledges: The Politics of Theory-Building and Pedagogy in Composition.* Albany, NY: State U of New York P, 1997.

Ede, Lisa. *Situating Composition: Composition Studies and the Politics of Location.* Carbondale: Southern Illinois UP, 2004.

Harkin, Patricia. "The Postdisciplinary Politics of Lore." *Contending with Words: Composition and Rhetoric in a Postmodern Age.* Ed. Patricia Harkin and John Schilb. New York: MLA, 1991. 124–38.

Johanek, Cindy. *Composing Research: A Contextualist Research Paradigm for Rhetoric and Composition.* Logan, UT: Utah State UP, 2000.

Phelps, Louise Wetherbee. *Composition as a Human Science: Contributions to the Self-Understanding of a Discipline.* New York: Oxford UP, 1988.

3 Genres in the Parlor: The Dissemination of Knowledge in Composition Studies

Just as there are multiple means by which knowledge in composition studies is constructed—through scholarship, empirical research, and practice—there are also multiple means by which knowledge in the discipline is disseminated. Like the modes of inquiry, the genres of the discipline offer important insights into how the conversation in the composition studies parlor is carried out. For example, knowledge in composition studies is shared through some common publication genres, such as books and journal articles; however, composition studies relies on these familiar genres in different ways than do many other disciplines. Also, in composition studies, knowledge is often publicized using genres that may be less prominent in other disciplines, such as position statements that are endorsed by professional organizations. Thus, before conducting bibliographic research, it is important that you understand how specific publication genres and other means of disseminating knowledge function uniquely in composition studies. This chapter will teach you what genres to investigate to ensure that your bibliographic project reflects the full range and depth of the discipline's knowledge about an issue. The information in this chapter will also help you to better assess each source you find in light of its genre's significance to the discipline.

BOOKS AND EDITED COLLECTIONS

Books are useful in composition studies because they provide a more comprehensive discussion than is possible in briefer publications, like journal articles. Another advantage of books as bibliographic sources is that most are readily obtained; if your university's library doesn't have a book that you need, you can usually borrow it from another academic library through your library's interlibrary loan service. Books also aid your later bibliographic searches by helping you identify specialists in your area of interest, helping you expand the keywords you may want to use for your bibliographic searches, and leading you to additional sources through the books' extensive bibliographies. Books are best located using catalogs, especially WorldCat, the most comprehensive catalog available, which is discussed in more detail in chapter five. CompPile, the major database for composition studies, also indexes books in the discipline, maintains a list of publishers of books in the discipline, and helps to draw attention to new books in the discipline through a separate listing of books published within the last two years; see the links for these lists at http://comppile.org.

There are two ways in which the use of books as a genre for disseminating disciplinary knowledge is unique in composition studies. First, based on his extensive analysis of published scholarship in composition studies, librarian Daniel Coffey reports that scholarly authors in the discipline generally include more citations to books than to any other genre of publication; however, authors also cite many other types of publication, so they do not cite books as exclusively as do scholarly authors of other disciplines. A second way in which books as a type of publication function uniquely in composition studies is that even though there are many single-author books, there is also a plethora of edited collections (books of essays by different authors about a common topic or theme). Each type of book has distinct advantages: books written entirely by one or two authors often impart more focused, complex, and sustained arguments, whereas edited collections offer a greater quantity and range of perspectives (Hawisher and Selfe 116).

In her essay "The Role of Edited Collections in Composition Studies," Laura Micciche identifies the reasons why edited collections are a common and valued genre of scholarship in composition studies. She writes that edited collections can often provide a greater breadth of knowledge than single-authored books because the essays in a collection frequently represent a diverse range of perspectives and methodologies. Also, collections often include work by known scholars as well as less familiar authors. Micciche sums up their value thusly: "edited collections present a unique opportunity to fulfill pedagogical functions by sketching the history and current state of a discipline, detailing new problems or issues from multiple perspectives, and by providing a site where minority voices can expand and challenge mainstream accounts of that same discipline" (107).

Micciche claims that the preponderance of edited collections in composition studies is in part due to the need for untenured faculty to publish while teaching a heavy load and/or administrating a writing program or writing center. A collection, she maintains, is a more manageable publication to produce than a single-authored book because the labor is shared. Gail Hawisher and Cynthia Selfe identify a different reason for the popularity of edited collections: "the genre seems especially critical to those fields we would label as relatively newly-constituted disciplines, such as cultural studies, film studies, literacy studies, and, we would argue, composition studies" (104). Whatever the reason for their popularity, edited collections are undoubtedly a major genre of scholarship in composition studies. In May 2009 (the most recent information available at the time of this writing), the CompPile database included 3,348 edited collections that had direct relevance to the discipline of composition studies.

A difficulty in bibliographic research involving edited collections is that while the titles of edited volumes are indexed in catalogs in the same manner as books, the titles of individual essays published in edited collections are not indexed in either catalogs or periodical databases. Most often, when you find an edited collection using a catalog, you will then need to examine the collection's table of contents (which may be part of the catalog record) in order to determine whether specific essays in the volume are particularly relevant to your research topic. The CompPile database is also tremendously helpful in bibliographic searches that involve edited collections because the essays in a collection are indexed individually. Therefore, you can locate a single relevant essay in an edited collection through a search of keywords related to your topic; also, by typing an edited collection's title in the search field for titles, you can retrieve a list of all the essays in that book. You will learn more about these and other features of the CompPile database in chapter five.

Whenever you rely on a book as a major source for your bibliographic project, whether it is single-authored or an edited collection, you should attempt to locate one or more published reviews of the book. Book reviews do more than help you to evaluate the book. As Mark Wiley explains in his article "How to Read a Book: Reflections on the Ethics of Book Reviewing," the best reviews are not simply an analysis of the book's strengths and weaknesses but are also an inquiry into how a particular book relates to concerns of the discipline. As a student learning the discipline, then, you should seek out reviews so that you better understand the disciplinary significance of books that you deem especially important to your bibliographic research project. Reviews are often published in peer-reviewed journals in the discipline and can be found by searching the book's title in a database that indexes periodicals; they currently are not routinely indexed in the CompPile database.

For Writing and Discussion

1. Go to the CompPile database homepage at http://comppile.org and under the heading labeled coverage, click to see the list of edited collections. Scan the many pages of edited collections and select one that seems relevant to the issue you are researching in composition studies. Next, return to the homepage and enter just the title of this edited collection in the "book" search field. This search will allow you to retrieve a list of all of the essays in the edited collection. Based on this brief exposure, in what ways do you think that edited collections will be useful in your bibliographic endeavors?

2. Read several book reviews of Stephen North's *The Making of Knowledge in Composition*. The full citations for reviews written by Richard Larson, Richard Lloyd-Jones, James Raymond, and Karen Spear are provided in the list of sources for further reading at the end of this chapter. Based on this exposure to book reviews, how do you think that book reviews can be helpful in your bibliographic endeavors? When multiple reviews of the same book are available, why might it be important to read more than one?

PRINT AND ELECTRONIC JOURNALS

The trait that most distinguishes scholarship in composition studies from scholarship in other disciplines in the social sciences and humanities is its heavy reliance on scholarly journals. Librarian Daniel Coffey provides evidence for this assertion with his citation analysis of scholarship in composition studies. A citation analysis is a method that academic librarians have devised for characterizing the scholarship of a discipline, often in order to make more informed decisions about how to allocate scarce library funds in ways that are most meaningful to students and faculty of various disciplines. To conduct a citation analysis, a librarian selects a large but representative sample of scholarship in a particular discipline, then tallies all of the citations in those publications according to the type of publication each citation represents: book, journal, essay in edited collection, or other material (a category that can include dissertations, theses, websites, email messages, or anything else that might appear in a source's list of references).

Librarian Daniel Coffey conducted his citation analysis of composition studies in order to investigate a claim made by compositionist John Schilb that scholarship in composition studies is "primarily article-driven" (27). To test this claim, Coffey selected the articles from five major composition journals, fifteen prominent single-authored books, and fifteen edited collections, all spanning a fourteen-year period, which provided a collective total of 41,281 citations. Coffey's analysis proved that as a discipline, composition studies relies much more on journals than do other disciplines.

In Coffey's analysis, 45% of the citations he analyzed referred to books, 30% were citations of journal articles, 20% were citations of essays in edited collections, and 5% were citations of other materials (the percentages here are rounded to the nearest whole number). Coffey cites previous citation studies that show other disciplines rely on journals much less; for example, a citation analysis of scholarship in literary studies showed that 76% of the citations were to books, only 13% were citations of journal articles, 8% were citations of essays in edited collections, and 3% were citations of other materials (again, the percentages are rounded). Coffey concludes that while publications in composition studies, like those of other disciplines, cite books most, "when viewed in comparison with other citation studies of humanities scholars, it becomes quite evident that journal articles are used to a much greater degree" in composition studies (161).

One reason why journal articles remain so vital in composition scholarship may be because journals were crucial to the development of the discipline. Both Robert Connors and Maureen Daly Goggin have published articles that trace how journals in composition studies fostered the growth of the discipline and defined its parameters. In

his essay, Connors discusses the first articles about composition published in the 1870s, the founding of the National Council of Teachers
of English in 1911 and the *English Journal* in 1912, and then the increasing proliferation of journals that followed: "By decades, then, the
thirties saw one journal founded, as did the forties. None appeared in
the fifties. Two were founded in the sixties, six journals were born in
the seventies, and thus far in the eighties [this article was published in
1984] we have seen five" (349). In the remainder of the article, Connors assesses all fifteen journals. Goggin's article, later expanded as
a book, chronicles the role of eight major journals in the discipline's
growth during the years 1950–1990. The number of journals in the
discipline continues to grow as the discipline does. There are now
more than forty journals, both print and online, in the discipline of
composition studies. In addition, in July 2008 (the latest information
available at the time of this writing), CompPile listed 306 journals that
have direct bearing on composition studies, and the CompPile editors
hope that the database will eventually index them all.

What is troublesome about journal articles in composition studies, especially given their importance to scholarship in the discipline,
is that the discipline's journals are not readily and equally available to
all members of the discipline. Libraries at institutions where there is a
large and long-standing graduate program in composition studies are
likely to own a sizable collection of journals, but smaller programs or
those established more recently will not. While most academic libraries provide access to the subscription-based databases that are recommended in chapter five, and while CompPile is available free of charge
on the internet, most of these databases typically provide only the citations of articles, not their full texts. Databases that include full texts
of articles are prohibitively expensive, so much so that libraries must
sometimes make the difficult decision to terminate their subscriptions
(see, for example, Foster's article in *The Chronicle of Higher Education*,
listed in the bibliography of this chapter).

A beacon of hope on the horizon is the open source movement,
which Peter Suber, editor of *Open Access News*, defines as having the
following goals: "Putting peer-reviewed scientific and scholarly literature on the internet. Making it available free of charge and free of most
copyright and licensing restrictions. Removing the barriers to serious
research." A small handful of composition journals currently follow
this model, notably *Across the Disciplines, Enculturation, Kairos, The*

WAC Journal, and *The Writing Instructor.* Other composition journals, such as *JAC, WPA: Writing Program Administration* and *Writing
Lab Newsletter,* have begun to offer full texts of all but the most recent issues on their websites, without charge, for subscribers and non-
subscribers alike. Charles Lowe's essay "Copyright, Access and Digital
Texts," an open access article itself (see the bibliography at the end of
this chapter for its web address), provides persuasive arguments and
additional suggestions for promoting open access to scholarly work.

Until such time as open access becomes the norm, students and
professionals in composition studies must make the most of the sources that are available. To assist you in finding full texts of the journal
articles you may need for your bibliographic project, Appendix B provides information about thirty-six scholarly journals in composition
and rhetoric, arranged alphabetically. Although this is not an exhaustive list of the journals in the field, all of the major journals are described. Also, all of these journals are refereed, meaning that articles
submitted for publication are subjected to a peer review process before
being accepted. I have excluded from this appendix journals no longer
being issued and those with a circulation of fewer than 400 (with the
exception of a few journals that focus on a narrow subspecialty of composition studies that may be highly relevant to some research interests).
I have also excluded many journals outside composition studies that
sometimes publish articles quite useful in composition studies, such as
Educational Researcher and *Radical Teacher.*

The description for each journal in Appendix B includes how frequently the journal is issued, when the journal began, and if available,
the journal's circulation. The circulation number identifies the number of subscribers to each journal at the time of this writing, which can
be useful in determining the journal's impact on the discipline. In addition, a description is provided that further characterizes the contents
of each journal. When additional information about the journal and
its contents can be located online, those web addresses are identified
and a description is provided of the features currently available on the
website. When possible, I have also identified in this appendix other
sites and databases that provide keyword searches and/or full text of
articles from the journal if these are not available on the journal's own
website.

Because disciplinary practices change quickly, particularly in
webbed environments, I must offer some important caveats about your

use of this information. Since the writing of these descriptions, websites may have changed, features may have been licensed to other reference services, and some journals may have ceased publication, while other new journals will have emerged. When a journal seems promising for your research interests, it is wise to check whether the information in its description is still current. Also, be aware that I have not listed all of the databases in which each journal is indexed, only the one or two that provide the fullest access (full texts are preferred) and that are likely to be widely available. If your library does not subscribe to a database I've named, you can use *Ulrich's Periodical Directory*, which may be available online through your library's website, to determine what other databases index the journal. For journals that do not have full text available online, or when the purchase price of an article seems too great, you may be able to obtain a copy of the article through your library's interlibrary loan services, although not all universities offer this service for journal articles.

For Writing and Discussion

1. Scan the names and descriptions of the thirty-six journals found in Appendix B. Next, access the CompPile homepage at http://comppile.org and under the "coverage" heading, click on journals and then on "sorted alphabetically," which will lead you to a page listing several hundred journals that have relevance for composition studies. In what ways is it useful to have the smaller list of journals located in Appendix B available for you to consult as you work on a bibliographic project? In what ways is it useful to have the much longer list of journals on CompPile available for you to consult as you work on a bibliographic project?

2. Appendix D is a table that allows you to record the journals related to composition studies that are owned by your campus library and other libraries near you. Using your library's online catalog, complete the table provided in Appendix D so that you will have a handy guide to the volumes of key journals in composition studies that are owned by your library. If there are other academic libraries near you that you can use, check their online catalogs also to determine if they own any journals that are not owned by your library; also, if your own cam-

pus's subscription to a journal is incomplete, determine whether the volumes missing from your own library's subscription can be found at another nearby library. Whenever you identify a promising journal article citation in a bibliography or database, you can then consult this table to quickly identify where you can obtain the article. (If you are completing this table as part of a class assignment, the completion of Appendix D is a task especially well suited for students to share.)

3. Familiarize yourself with the open access movement by reading Peter Suber's "Open Access Overview," available at http://www. earlham.edu/~peters/fos/overview.htm. In what ways might an increase in open access literature change bibliographic projects? In what ways might an increase in open access literature change the production of knowledge in composition studies?

THESES AND DISSERTATIONS

Another means by which knowledge in composition studies is shared is through theses and dissertations, the culminating documents that graduate students are required to write for their master's or doctoral degree. Theses and dissertations span the modes of inquiry used to construct knowledge in composition studies: most are primarily scholarly attempts to address issues in the discipline; many report the methods, data, and findings of an empirical research project in composition studies; a few may even be primarily practical knowledge. Although typically theses and dissertations are not widely distributed, their abstracts alone can be useful. Chapter five will discuss databases useful in locating thesis and dissertation abstracts. Dissertations relevant to composition studies are also indexed in CompPile, and more detailed abstracts of theses and dissertations in composition studies, organized topically and listed in reverse chronological order, are provided on the WAC Clearinghouse website at http://wac.colostate.edu/theses/ (click "view details" next to each heading to obtain the full bibliographic information for each text).

For Writing and Discussion

1. Explore the dissertation abstracts posted on the WAC Clearinghouse website at http://wac.colostate.edu/theses. After reading several of the abstracts available on this site, how would you describe the role that dissertations and theses play in the production and sharing of knowledge in composition studies?

2. Is one of the content areas listed on the website http://wac.colostate.edu/theses related to the topic you have chosen for your bibliographic project? If so, read the dissertation titles and several of the abstracts that address this topic. To what extent do you think dissertations and theses can be helpful to your bibliographic project?

PROFESSIONAL ORGANIZATIONS' WEBSITES, POSITION STATEMENTS, AND CONVENTIONS

There are many professional organizations that advance knowledge in the discipline of composition studies. The largest of these organizations is the National Council of Teachers of English (NCTE), which has over 60,000 members, including English language arts educators and administrators at all levels of education, from elementary school through the university. NCTE also has several constituent organizations; the one devoted to composition studies in higher education is the Conference on College Composition and Communication (CCCC). Within CCCC there are also special interest groups and assemblies, such as the Conference on Basic Writing (CBW) and the International Writing Centers Association (IWCA). There are also professional organizations related to composition studies that have no formal affiliation with NCTE, such as the Council of Writing Program Administrators (CWPA) and the International Network of Writing-across-the-Curriculum Programs (INWAC).

One of the ways that these professional organizations disseminate knowledge about composition studies is through resources provided on the organizations' websites. For example, the IWCA's site, located at http://writingcenters.org/index.php, provides links with information on starting a writing center, peer tutoring in writing, directing a writing center, and online writing labs (OWLs), among other topics. The

WAC Clearinghouse website, affiliated with INWAC and located at
http://wac.colostate.edu/, provides extensive resources about writing-
across-the-curriculum, including bibliographies, links, and program
descriptions. The CWPA site, located at http://www.wpacouncil.org/,
offers links to the websites of hundreds of writing programs at colleges
and universities, detailed models of writing assessment at a range of
institutions, information on consultant-evaluator services for writing
programs, and other valuable information.

Many professional organizations also develop, ratify, and post on
their websites position statements and guidelines that serve as national standards of professional practice. The largest number of position
statements has been developed by NCTE. The full list is available at
http://www.ncte.org/positions; the position statements address matters
such as assessment and testing, classroom size and workload, beliefs
about writing, diversity, grammar, and working conditions. Examples
of recent position statements include "NCTE-WPA White Paper on
Writing Assessment in Colleges and Universities," "CCCC Statement
on the Multiple Uses of Writing," "Principles and Practices in Electronic Portfolios," "The NCTE Statement on 21st-Century Literacies,"
and "NCTE Position Paper on the Role of English Teachers in Edu-
cating English Language Learners (ELLs)." Additional position statements developed by the Council of Writing Program Administrators
can be found on the CWPA website at http://www.wpacouncil.org/
positions/index.html. The "WPA Outcomes Statement for First-Year
Composition," for example, seeks to "regularize what can be expected
to be taught in first-year composition." Among other position statements, CWPA also offers "Defining and Avoiding Plagiarism: The
WPA Statement on Best Practices." Because all position statements are
written collaboratively, are rigorously discussed, and typically require
a vote of approval from the organization's membership or its Executive
Committee, you can have confidence when citing position statements
in your bibliographic projects that they reflect well the goals and beliefs of the discipline, not the idiosyncrasies of individuals.

A final way in which professional organizations contribute to the
production and dissemination of knowledge in composition studies is
by hosting annual conferences or conventions. At these conventions,
members of the organization and others interested in composition
studies gather to hear plenary speakers and to orally deliver papers
in concurrent sessions. Often, longer workshops that contribute to

professional development are offered at the convention site just before and after the conference. In your bibliographic research, you can access some conference papers through the ERIC database (discussed in more detail in chapter five).

For Writing and Discussion

1. Starting at the CompPile homepage at http://comppile.org, click on several of the links for professional organizations in composition studies. What kinds of resources are available on these organizations' websites? How might these websites be useful to your bibliographic project?

2. Look at the list of NCTE position statements available at http://www.ncte.org/positions, as well as those by the Council of Writing Program Administrators, available at http://www.wpa-council.org/positions/index.html. How might position statements be useful to your bibliographic project?

3. If you have not attended a professional conference in composition studies, looking at programs from past conferences can help you to better understand the magnitude and range of topics discussed by presenters and other participants. You can look at some past CCCC programs at http://www.ncte.org/cccc/review; programs and abstracts for some past International WAC conferences are available at http://wac.colostate.edu/proceedings/. After browsing several of these programs, how would you describe the role that professional conferences play in the production and dissemination of knowledge in composition studies? To what extent might conference papers be useful to your bibliographic project?

MAILING LISTS AND THEIR ARCHIVES

A final way that knowledge in composition studies is shared is through online mailing lists. Even though these lists are often affiliated with a professional organization, I have separated them from the above section about organizations' means of sharing disciplinary knowledge because mailing lists are almost entirely user-driven. Subscribers sometimes use the list to request referrals to scholarly work or to recommend a scholarly source, but most often the information shared on mailing lists is practical knowledge, including exchanges about institutional practices.

There are numerous mailing lists for composition studies, each serving a unique specialization or area of interest. Some of the lists are WPA-L (a very active list about writing program administration but also many other topics related to composition studies), H-Rhetor (about the history of rhetoric; this list began in August 1993, making it probably the oldest mailing list in the discipline), WCenter (about writing centers and tutoring), and WAC-L (about writing across the curriculum). Links to these and other mailing lists are available at http://rhetcomp.com/ and (forthcoming) on the CompPile homepage.

Many mailing lists provide searchable archives of past messages, which can sometimes be useful for bibliographic projects. Searching archives, however, can be challenging because the people who post messages may not use the expected search terms in their subject headings. Also, a string of posts may retain the same subject line even when the topic shifts. Searching mailing list archives, then, involves much more trial and error (and frankly, luck) than does searching a database. In rare instances, it may be appropriate to cite a message that has been posted on a mailing list, but because subscribers generally intend their emails to have a short duration, list archives are best used for noting common trends in practice and for finding leads to other quotable sources.

For Writing and Discussion

1. What questions do you have about the issue in composition studies you are investigating that a mailing list might help you to answer?

2. Browse the links to mailing lists that are available at http://rhetcomp.com/ or at the CompPile homepage, http://comppile.org. Which mailing list is likely to have the greatest relevance to the topic you have chosen for your bibliographic project? What process should be used to search the archives for this mailing list?

If the discipline of composition studies can be compared to a parlor room, this chapter has shown that the parlor is quite large, with lots of nooks for smaller conversation groups. It will take quite some time

for you to explore the full room, with all that the discipline has to offer. As you begin your bibliographic work, though, it's important to
keep the full dimensions of the room in mind. Consider how the issue
in composition studies that you are investigating can be informed by
each mode of knowledge: scholarship, empirical research, and practical knowledge. Also consider how your bibliographic research can be
enhanced by the full range of ways in which knowledge is shared in
the discipline, not only single-authored books, but also edited collections, journal articles, dissertations, professional organizations' website
resources, organizations' position statements, conference papers, and
mailing list archives. Now that you have this fuller context for work
in the discipline, the remaining chapters of this book will lead you
through the process for undertaking a bibliographic research project:
the preparatory steps for conducting a bibliographic search (chapter
four), the databases and bibliographic resources you should consult
(chapter five), and the steps for completing bibliographic assignments.

WORKS CITED

Coffey, Daniel P. "A Discipline's Composition: A Citation Analysis of Composition Studies." *The Journal of Academic Librarianship* 32 (2006): 155–
65.

Connors, Robert J. "Journals in Composition Studies." *College English* 46
(1984): 348–65.

Foster, Andrea L. "Second Thoughts on 'Bundled E-Journals.'" *The Chronicle of Higher Education* 49.4 (September 20, 2002): A31. 20 September
2008 <http://chronicle.com/free/v49/i04/04a03101.htm>.

Goggin, Maureen Daly. "Composing a Discipline: The Role of Scholarly
Journals in the Disciplinary Emergence of Rhetoric and Composition
Since 1950." *Rhetoric Review* 15 (1997): 322–48.

Hawisher, Gail E., and Cynthia L. Selfe. "The Edited Collection: A Scholarly Contribution and More." *Publishing in Rhetoric and Composition*. Ed.
Gary A. Olson and Todd W. Taylor. Albany, NY: SUNY Press, 1997.
103–18.

Lowe, Charles. "Copyright, Access, and Digital Texts." *Across the Disciplines* 1 (2004). 9 September 2008 <http://wac.colostate.edu/atd/articles/
lowe2003/>.

Micciche, Laura. "The Role of Edited Collections in Composition Studies."
Composition Forum 12 (2001): 101–24.

Schilb, John. "Scholarship in Composition and Literature: Some Compari-
sons." *Academic Advancement in Composition Studies: Scholarship, Publi-*

cation, Promotion, Tenure. Ed. Richard C. Gebhardt and Barbara Genelle Smith Gebhardt. Mahwah, NJ: Lawrence Erlbaum, 1997. 21–30.

Suber, Peter. *Open Access News: News from the Open Access Movement.* 9 September 2008 <http://www.earlham.edu/%7Epeters/fos/fosblog.html>.

Wiley, Mark. "How to Read a Book: Reflections on the Ethics of Book Reviewing." *JAC: Journal of Advanced Composition* 13 (1993): 477–92.

"WPA Outcomes Statement for First-Year Composition." April 2000. Council of Writing Program Administrators. 27 August 2008 <http://wpa-council.org/book/export/html/8>.

For Further Reading

"About SPARC." *SPARC: The Scholarly Publishing and Academic Resources Coalition.* 6 September 2008 <http://www.arl.org/sparc/about/index.shtml>.

Day, Michael. "A Meshing of Minds: The Future of Online Research for Print and Electronic Publication?" *New Worlds, New Words: Exploring Pathways for Writing about and in Electronic Environments.* Ed. John F. Barber and Dene Grigar. Cresskill, NJ: Hampton P, 2001. 251–77.

Gale, Fredric G. "Composition Journals and the Politics of Knowledge-Making: A Conversation with Journal Editors." *JAC: Journal of Advanced Composition* 18 (1998): 197–211.

Gebhardt, Richard C. "Refereed Publication in Composition Studies and CCC." *Rhetoric Review* 13 (1995): 238–44.

Goggin, Maureen. *Authoring a Discipline: Scholarly Journals and the Post-World War II Emergence of Rhetoric and Composition.* Mahwah, NJ: Erlbaum, 2000.

Hunter, Susan. "The Case for Reviewing as Collaboration and Response." *Rhetoric Review* 13 (1995): 265–72.

Information Access Alliance. 6 September 2008 <http://www.information-access.org>.

Larson, Richard L. Untitled review of *The Making of Knowledge in Composition: Portrait of an Emerging Field* by Stephen M. North. *College Composition and Communication* 40 (1989): 95–98.

Lloyd-Jones, Richard. Untitled review of *The Making of Knowledge in Composition: Portrait of an Emerging Field* by Stephen M. North. *College Composition and Communication* 40 (1989): 98–100.

Lunsford, Andrea, and Susan West. "Intellectual Property and Composition Studies." *College Composition and Communication* 47 (1996): 383–411.

Luzon, Maria Jose. "The Added Value Features of Online Scholarly Journals." *Journal of Technical Writing and Communication* 27 (2007): 59–73.

Raymond, James C. Untitled review of *The Making of Knowledge in Composition: Portrait of an Emerging Field* by Stephen M. North. *College Composition and Communication* 40 (1989): 93–95.

Spear, Karen I. Untitled book review of *The Making of Knowledge in Composition: Portrait of an Emerging Field* by Stephen M. North. *JAC: Journal of Advanced Composition* 9 (1989). 9 September 2008 <http://www.jacweb. org/Archived_volumes/Text_articles/V9_Rev_Spear.htm>.

Willinsky, John. *The Access Principle: The Case for Open Access to Research and Scholarship.* Cambridge, MA: MIT Press, 2006.

4 Approaching the Parlor's Threshold: Preparing for Your Bibliographic Search in Composition Studies

From the previous chapters, you have become acquainted with the parlor of composition studies, specifically, the modes of inquiry used to generate knowledge in the discipline and the genres that are used to disseminate that knowledge. Now that you better understand how the conversation in the discipline takes place, you are ready to cross the threshold into the discipline's parlor and begin to research an issue in composition studies.

This chapter will guide you through some preliminary tasks that can improve the effectiveness and efficiency of your search for scholarly sources in composition studies. With the assistance provided in this chapter, you will learn how to assess the composition-related resources that are available at your university's library and at other libraries available to you. You will also decide what search terms best represent your research interest so that your online searches can produce the most relevant results. Additionally, you will learn how to refine your search for sources by using Boolean operators and advanced search options, as well as how to keep track of your searches. You will decide too upon the criteria you will use to select sources from your search results. Lastly, you will choose a documentation style so that you can accurately record the citations for the sources you find. The exercises throughout this chapter will help you with each of these preparatory steps.

ASSESSING YOUR LIBRARY'S RESOURCES

The success of your bibliographic research in composition studies depends upon not only your knowledge of bibliographic research methods but also the library resources available to you. For that reason, it can be time well spent to begin your bibliographic research project by assessing the library resources at your disposal. Even if you are already familiar with your academic library because you have used it to complete work assigned in prior courses, chances are you have not thoroughly analyzed your library's strengths and weaknesses, particularly as they pertain to bibliographic research in composition studies. You will be better able to manage the time allocated to you for a bibliographic project if you determine in advance what research can be done online and what must be done on the library's premises, as well as what challenges you may face in obtaining copies of the sources you will need and the extent to which you may need to access other libraries.

Appendix A in this book provides an extensive list of questions you can use to identify and evaluate the library resources in composition studies that are available to you. Specifically, these questions guide you in determining your access to your university library's resources online and in person, its collection of books and journals related to composition studies, its subscription to databases useful for bibliographic research in composition studies, and its interlibrary loan services. The appendix also includes questions about other academic libraries and public libraries you may be able to use. If you are reading this text for a course, your professor may want to assign the questions in Appendix A as a collaborative project, so students can divide the questions and then pool their responses for the benefit of everyone.

IDENTIFYING YOUR SEARCH TERMS

A crucial step in preparing for a bibliographic search is to identify the terms you will search online that best represent your research interests. You'll need a variety of potential search terms because the terms that work well for one database may not work well for another. This section explains the two main types of search terms: keywords and controlled vocabulary.

Keywords

Keywords are words you choose because you think they best represent your research topic. Keywords can be single words or word phrases. There are a few tricks you should learn for representing each in an online search. A single keyword can usually be simply typed into a search box, but some databases also support a truncation function that allows you to replace the ending of a word with a symbol (the most common symbol is * but some databases use the symbol ! or ?). By typing the root of a word and then a truncation symbol, you are able to search all forms of the word in a database simultaneously. For example, the truncated keyword "collaborat*" would yield results that include collaborate, collaborating, collaborated, collaborative, and collaboration. Truncation symbols can also be helpful when your search might include both singular and plural forms of a word. Most databases will have a "Help" or "Examples" guide that identifies which truncation symbol that database uses.

When your keyword is a phrase, you need to type it so that the database recognizes your search entry as a phrase. Do this by surrounding the words with quotation marks or with parentheses. For example, someone who is researching service learning should type the keyword phrase into the search box as "service learning" or (service learning); otherwise, the search results may include sources that contain the words "service" and "learning" even if the words are not used in conjunction with each other.

Knowing how to represent keywords and keyword phrases in an online search is just the beginning of knowing how to use keywords well. Your bibliographic search can be successful only if your keywords are accurate, comprehensive, and specific. To be accurate, your keywords must convey your research interest using the same terminology used by scholars in composition studies. Suppose, for example, that you want to research an issue affecting college students who receive low scores on the placement test used to assign them to a college writing course. If you used the search term "remedial writers" to describe such students, you would not be able to locate much of the scholarship that has been published about these students because most composition scholars refer to such students using the terms "basic writers" or "developmental writers." It is critical, then, that you be knowledgeable about the discipline-specific terms used to describe issues in composition studies and that you use these terms accurately when searching for sources online. Two books that serve as introductions to the terms used by composition scholars are Babin and Harrison's *Contemporary Composition Studies: A Guide to Theorists and Terms* and Heilker and Vandenberg's *Keywords in Composition Studies;* the full citations of both books are provided in the bibliography at the end of this chapter.

In addition to being accurate, the keywords you select must be comprehensive. In other words, your bibliographic search will often be more successful if you search multiple synonyms for each keyword. For instance, the process of students meeting in groups to exchange comments on each other's drafts might be variously referred to in composition scholarship as group work, peer critique, peer evaluation, peer feedback, peer groups, peer response, peer review, peer writing groups, response groups, small group work, student writing groups, and writing workshops, among other possibilities. If you were researching this topic and selected only one of these terms as a keyword to search, you would find only a small portion of the scholarly writing about your topic. Similarly, what might once have been an adequate search with just the keyword phrase "English as a second language" or its acronym "ESL" should now also include keyword searches for "ELL" (English language learners), "L2 writers," "generation 1.5 students" and "second language writing," among others.

Another consideration in ensuring that search terms are comprehensive is that you must have multiple search terms for every aspect of your research interest. For example, if you wish to find scholarly publications about the effectiveness of peer response groups for second language writers, all of the aforementioned keywords should be considered. As you begin to research and read more about your topic, you may encounter still more potential keywords that you haven't yet searched. Remember that it is never too late to add keywords to enhance your search for bibliographic sources.

Finally, while you should strive to be comprehensive in your keywords so that you do not miss relevant sources, you should also strive to make your keywords specific enough that they will not generate hundreds or even thousands of search results. Such results are time-consuming to sort through, and it is easy to become frustrated when the vast majority of the search results are irrelevant to your research interests. Consider a keyword as fundamental to the discipline as "composition." Databases that index numerous journals in composition studies—journals in which "composition" refers to writing—may also index journals in other disciplines that use the term "composition" differently; for example, search results may refer to a musical composition or to the molecular composition of an object being studied scientifically. Even terms that seem much narrower than "composition" can generate scores of irrelevant search results. For example, many of the sources that are identified using keywords previously recommended for describing students' critiques of each other's writing—such as "peer response" and "peer review"—may be entirely irrelevant if the resulting citations do not use these keywords within the context of composition studies. Often, the best strategy for increasing the number of relevant search results is to enter multiple keywords and search them simultaneously. When the keywords are searched in combination, the desired definition of each keyword is clarified, and irrelevant search results are lessened.

Controlled Vocabulary

Some databases index sources using a controlled vocabulary rather than keywords. Controlled vocabulary is the name given to search terms that have been predetermined by the staff who manage the database. To successfully search a database that uses a controlled vocabulary, you must use the database's predetermined search terms—sometimes called subject headings or descriptors—rather than your own keywords. The advantage of databases that use controlled vocabularies is that once you identify the database's controlled vocabulary for your topic, you can be confident that a search of that term will yield comprehensive results. You do not need to conduct multiple searches in the database using numerous possible keyword synonyms for your research interest.

Databases that use controlled vocabularies typically provide a reference tool such as a thesaurus or glossary to help you identify the search terms used to describe your research interest in that database. For example, the thesaurus of the *MLA International Bibliography,* a major database for composition studies, identifies "student writers" as the search term one should use when searching this database for sources about composition students; "writing centers" is the recommended search term for sources about writing labs; and "writing apprehension" is the search term that will yield the best results for sources about writing anxiety. Remember that the controlled vocabulary for any given database will often differ from the controlled vocabulary in another database, so it is important to separately identify the search terms used in each database that has a controlled vocabulary. Also, realize that any search term that a database identifies as its controlled vocabulary can also serve as a keyword you may wish to search in a database that does not use a controlled vocabulary.

For Writing and Discussion

1. Prepare a list of keywords to use when searching for scholarly publications about the issue in composition studies you want to investigate. Be sure to designate a keyword for every aspect of your research interest: the general and the more specific topics of your inquiry, and if appropriate, the types of students (grade level, ability level, etc.) you intend to study. Try your best to identify keywords that are accurate terminology in the field of composition studies. Then, because each keyword will have varying degrees of success in different databases, expand your list of possible keywords by writing several synonyms for each.

2. Once you have generated a list of keywords for your research interest that is accurate, comprehensive, and specific, seek feedback on your list from other people who read scholarly publications in composition studies, including classmates and faculty. What keywords do they recommend that you add?

3. To better understand how controlled vocabularies aid in a database search, explore the glossary for the online database CompPile, located at http://comppile.org/site/glossary.htm. What types of help with search terms does this glossary provide? What search terms are used in CompPile to represent your research interest, according to this glossary? What are the search terms that you might expect to represent your topic, yet the CompPile glossary indicates that they are excluded from this database? Are any of these excluded words ones that you can add to your list of keywords to search in other databases?

4. In order to contrast the controlled vocabularies of different databases, consult the thesaurus tool of the database *MLA International Bibliography,* a database that must be accessed through your campus library's website. Once you have logged on to this database, click on the thesaurus link on the toolbar near the top of the screen, type a keyword for your research topic into the thesaurus search box, and browse the results. Do the search words used for your topic in this database differ from the search terms recommended by the CompPile glossary? Explore the features of this thesaurus, including the ability to click on terms to explode the search terms to find broader and

narrower search terms, to select the term as a major concept so that the search will retrieve only sources in which that term is prominent, and to combine multiple terms to search them simultaneously. If necessary, consult the database's help feature to better understand these thesaurus functions. In what ways are the thesaurus features of this database more or less helpful than the glossary features of CompPile?

Understanding Web Search Options

Understanding your options when searching online will enable you to search more effectively. You can eliminate many inappropriate search findings by knowing how to use Boolean operators and how to set search limits using advanced search options. These skills will save you time because they decrease the number of irrelevant search results, ensuring that a greater proportion of the search results match your research interests.

Boolean Operators

Most search engines and databases allow you to improve your search results by using Boolean operators. Boolean operators are single words that are typed in all capital letters between search terms to explain the relationship between those search terms. One Boolean operator is AND. Use it between search terms when you want to search for only the sources that include all of your search terms, as in this example: "service learning" AND "basic writers." Another Boolean operator is OR. Use it between search terms when you want the results to include any of your search terms. It's an especially helpful operator to use between keyword synonyms, as in this search example: "basic writers" OR "developmental writers." A final Boolean operator that's useful to know is NOT. Use it between search terms when you want to exclude certain results. For example, this search—"writing assessment" NOT holistic—would return results that discuss other forms of writing assessment but not holistic scoring. Boolean operators are provided as explicit options on many databases, but even when they are not prominently displayed you can use them by simply typing them into a search box window along with your search terms.

Advanced Search Options

Many databases offer both basic and advanced search options. To perform an advanced search, you usually must click on a link from the basic search screen in order to open a more sophisticated search page. Advanced search pages vary in the options they provide, but most provide multiple search boxes that make it easier to search several keywords simultaneously. Another important feature of advanced searches is the ability to set limits on your results. You can often limit your results to particular years, to particular languages, to particular types of publications (such as books or articles), to only those sources in peer-reviewed publications, and so on. Yet another very helpful feature of many advanced searches is the ability to select how your results will be sorted. You can choose whether you'd like the results to be shown to you so that the most recently published sources appear first, or whether you'd like the results organized so that those most relevant to your search appear first. Whenever you begin to work with a new database in doing your bibliographic search, explore its advanced search page to discover what options it provides in letting you refine your search.

Search Histories

Now that you have identified multiple search terms and have read about the ways in which search terms can be combined when searching online, you can understand why it is easy to lose track of what combinations you have already tried. Many databases allow you to view your search history within that database, but you will have no record of what searches you have conducted in multiple databases. For that reason, I recommend that you prepare a chart like the one illustrated here to track your search attempts. This table is just a sample of the format: your completed search log should be many rows longer than this abbreviated search log.

Table 1: Sample Search Log

Search Terms Used	Database	Comments

This search log can help you to avoid repeating searches you have already conducted. The first column is where you can record the terms you have searched; the entries in this column should be written identically to what you enter in a search box, including the truncation symbols, quotation marks around keyword phrases, and any Boolean operators you have used. In the second column, record which database you used when performing this search. You can also indicate in this column whether you used the basic or advanced search page of the database, and if you used the latter, you can note what limits you set. The third column prompts you to briefly comment on the success of each search in ways that will help you to refine your later searches. For example, if a search results in excessive sources, your comment might read "400 hits; need to narrow." For searches that identify a reasonable number of sources, including several sources highly relevant to your research interest that you haven't found in previous searches, a simple comment like "4 great finds" will remind you to repeat this combination of keywords in another database. Occasionally when reading through your search results, you may notice some words you haven't considered that seem to have good potential as search terms. Using a search log enables you to jot down these search terms in a subsequent row so that you do not forget them and to then continue with your current search.

For Writing and Discussion

1. To better understand the differences between basic and advanced search pages, explore both for one database, the *MLA International Bibliography,* available through your university library's website. This is the same database for which you may have already examined the thesaurus (as directed by a previous exercise in this chapter), but this time you will be examining the database's search pages. Though both the basic and advanced search pages of this database offer options for refining your search, the advanced search page offers more of these options and also allows you to designate the field (author, title, etc.) of each search term. Choose two or more of the keywords you found in the MLA thesaurus that represent your research topic and search this combination of keywords using first the basic search page; then click on the "advanced search" tab and enter the same keywords, using the additional options available on this page to refine your search. Compare the results produced by your basic and advanced searches, particularly the quantity and relevancy of the search results. Keeping in mind that the differences between basic and advanced search pages will differ for each database, what has your examination of this one database taught you about the possible benefits of advanced search options?

2. Create a three-column search log like the one illustrated in this chapter that you can use to track your bibliographic search attempts. In the keyword column, record some possible combinations of keywords you plan to search. Be sure to write the keywords exactly as they will be searched, with any truncation symbols, quotation marks around phrases, and Boolean operators you will use when you conduct your searches. You do not

need to conduct the searches of these terms until you have read more about the databases most helpful to composition studies, explained in chapter five. Remember, however, that varying even one of your search terms in a given database will yield different results, as will searching through all the search term combinations again in a different database. If you are using this book in a course, your professor may assign you to submit your completed search log, identifying all of your searches and the databases you have used, as evidence of the comprehensiveness of your search efforts.

Establishing Your Criteria for Sources

No matter how carefully you have chosen your search terms and used options that allow you to refine your searches, you will undoubtedly locate many more sources than you need for your project, including many sources that are irrelevant or otherwise inappropriate. Thus, it's essential when preparing for bibliographic research that you identify the criteria you will use to select from your search results those sources you want to read and study.

Quantity

Quantity alone might seem like a superficial criterion for bibliographic research; it's not how many sources you've included that matters, but what those sources say, right? Yet you cannot claim to have a comprehensive understanding of a topic if you have not read about the topic extensively and from multiple authors' perspectives. Estimating the quantity of sources you will need for your bibliographic project can also help you to better determine how selective you should be when gleaning sources from your search results.

If you are compiling an annotated bibliography or writing a paper for a course, your professor may assign the minimum number of sources that are required for your assignment. If no required number of sources is assigned and you need to estimate the number of sources you will need, base your decision on the breadth and complexity of your topic as well as on the length of your written project. A paper that is one of several shorter papers in a course will require fewer sources than a major seminar paper that is the basis for much of your course grade. A thesis or dissertation provides a more exhaustive examination of a topic than a course paper, so readers' expectations about the quantity of sources you cite in these manuscripts are far greater. Whatever number of sources you determine is an appropriate goal for your written project, strive to exceed that number by roughly one-third for your bibliographic search. By locating more sources than you expect to need, you will have the leeway to dismiss any sources that are less helpful than you expected once you have read them, either because they discuss your topic too briefly or because they merely replicate what is better stated in other sources.

Credibility

An important criterion for the sources you select should be whether those sources are considered credible by readers who are specialists in composition studies. To be credible to such readers, sources must be informed by composition theory and must be written for academics, not general readers; that is, the sources you select should be scholarly. The easiest way to ensure your sources are credible is to use only academic libraries and their databases when searching for sources. Academic libraries and databases have their own rigorous criteria for selecting sources, so the sources you find through these means will likely be from reputable publishing houses and peer-reviewed journals. You won't then need to sort through your search results to determine which readings lack scholarly rigor. The databases and websites that are best for locating scholarship in composition studies are identified in chapter five of this book. If your topic is interdisciplinary, you will need to consult databases and journals beyond those recommended in this text. You may be able to choose the best discipline-specific databases you need by consulting the descriptions of databases that are posted on your library's website; however, if you need additional help with databases designed for other fields, you can ask a reference librarian at your academic library for assistance. For all bibliographic research, restrict your use of publicly available search engines like Google and Yahoo to searches for information about institutional and curricular practice, and perhaps to locate the websites of professional organizations that are related to your research topic.

Relevance

Another criterion for the sources you select should be whether the source is relevant to your research interest. A source's title will help you make this decision, but many databases also provide abstracts, which can be even more useful as you decide upon a source's relevancy. Be aware as you examine the sources identified through a search that relevancy is a matter of degree. While sources that have no relevancy to your research interests can be easily dismissed, it is unrealistic to expect that every source you select will discuss all aspects of your topic fully. You may find many sources that discuss just one of your keywords and are thus partially relevant, while there may be only a few sources—or perhaps even none—that address every element of your topic thoroughly. Be careful, then, not to be overly selective when determining a source's relevancy. Strive to locate sources that provide a substantial discussion of even one aspect of your topic, and examine these in conjunction with other sources that discuss the remaining aspects of your research interest.

Timeliness

The date of the publication is another important criterion for selecting sources. If the topic of your research would be served by historical inquiry, you should of course include many decidedly older sources, but even if your research interest is not primarily historical, it can still be useful to include a few older sources that were influential in shaping the field's knowledge about the topic you are researching. You can best judge the merits of older sources by examining the bibliographies of recent sources; those older sources that are included in the bibliographies of numerous recent publications about your topic are likely to be historically significant. Another resource for identifying historically significant sources on your topic is a series of books whose titles all begin *Landmark Essays on* [various topics such as basic writing, ESL writing, the writing process, writing centers, advanced composition, etc.], published in the 1990s and early 2000s by Hermagoras Press.

Unless you are researching an historical person, practice, or concept related to composition studies, the vast majority of your sources should be published rather recently. Sources published within the last ten or fifteen years will best represent the field's current knowledge about your topic. If your topic is one that is especially time sensitive, such as one related to technology or to a recent pedagogical or curricular trend, you may need to ensure that your research is bibliographically current by selecting mostly sources published within the last three to five years.

Cumulative Merit

A final criterion you should consider when selecting sources is the cumulative merit of all your sources. To be considered comprehensive, your bibliography should be comprised of various types of publication, including books, articles from different journals, and, when relevant, other sources such as position statements from professional organizations. If a topic you are researching is controversial, make sure that differing perspectives are represented in your selection of sources. You need not agree with all the sources you cite, but you do need to understand the contentions at stake, and you may wish to discuss some sources in order to refute them. Also, consider the usefulness of including sources that represent a variety of approaches to disciplinary knowledge: theoretical discussions, historical accounts, scholarly criticism, reports of empirical studies, and descriptions of practice. If your research interest is interdisciplinary, your sources should include ones in composition studies as well as relevant sources recognized as credible in other pertinent academic fields. In judging whether your bibliography is comprehensive, also consider the range and overall currency your sources' publication dates; as previously discussed, unless your research is primarily historical, most dates should be recent but some sources with historical significance should also be included. Also examine the length of your sources; brief articles can be included, but the majority should be longer than ten pages. Finally, if your research is an examination of the relationship between several subtopics, make sure that the number of sources in your bibliography about each subtopic is correctly proportionate to the importance of those subtopics in your research.

For Writing and Discussion

1. Approximately how many sources do you expect to need for your current bibliographic research project? Now, increase your initial estimate by at least one-third, which will allow you to later omit the sources that are less promising than you expected. What is your revised estimate for the number of sources you must find?

2. Does your research topic encompass several distinct subtopics? If so, what are they? Based on the relative importance of each

subtopic to your research, approximately how many sources do you think you will need to find about each subtopic?

3. Does your research topic depend on scholarship published in disciplines other than composition studies? If so, identify these disciplines, then estimate the proportion of scholarly sources you will need from each to thoroughly investigate your research topic. How many of your total number of sources should be sources that are published in composition studies? How many should be sources published in each of these other disciplines? How do you plan to identify the best scholarly databases for these other disciplines?

4. How important is an historical perspective to your research topic? Approximately how many sources published prior to fifteen years ago do you expect to need? Can you identify the eras or former decades that you want those sources to represent? If your topic is particularly time sensitive (for example, a topic related to technology), how many sources do you hope to find that have been published within the last three to five years?

5. In addition to the criteria discussed in this chapter for selecting sources—quantity, credibility, relevance, timeliness, and cumulative merit—what other criteria can you think of that may help you select sources for your project from your bibliographic searches?

Choosing a Documentation Style

Scholarly work in composition studies generally uses one of two documentation styles: MLA or APA. Rarely will you have the opportunity to choose which documentation style you prefer because a particular style is usually required by a professor, a university's Graduate College (if you are writing a thesis or dissertation), an editor, or a publisher. Nevertheless, it's wise to determine which style you will use for your citations before you begin your research so that as you find sources, you can record all the information you need for that documentation style and can format the citations correctly.

Both styles have far too many nuances to explain here, so it's important that you obtain a copy of the style manual you intend to use for your research project and keep it handy for easy reference. The MLA and APA styles differ greatly in how the information in a citation is sequenced (especially the placement of publication dates) and in how citations are formatted (especially the use of capitalization and punctuation). There are also crucial differences in how you should cite sources within your prose, depending on which style you are using.

MLA

MLA documentation is the documentation style endorsed by the Modern Language Association. MLA style is used most often for scholarship done in English studies, including the majority of theoretical and historical scholarship published in composition studies. There are two authoritative guidebooks that explain how to use MLA style. *MLA Style Manual and Guide to Scholarly Publishing,* published in its third edition in 2008, explains MLA style conventions for graduate students, scholars, and professional writers. A separate guide, *MLA Handbook for Writers of Research Papers,* published in its seventh edition in 2009, is more appropriate for high school students and undergraduates. You can learn if more recent editions of these guides have been published by checking the Modern Languages Association website at http://www.mla.org (click the "Publications" tab).

APA

APA documentation is the style endorsed by the American Psychological Association. Although its use in composition studies is less common, it is the style most commonly used in reports of empirical studies done in composition studies, including those published in the journals *Research in the Teaching of English* and *Written Communication.* APA style is explained in *Publication Manual of the American Psychological Association,* most recently published in its sixth edition in 2010. APA also publishes the text *Mastering APA Style: Student's Workbook and Training Guide* (2010) for those who would like more practice with this style. You can learn if more recent editions of these guides have been published by checking the American Psychological Association website, http://www.apa.org (look for a link to "APA Style").

Reference Management Software

Until recently, writers had no choice but to format citations manually, yet now many reference management software programs exist that organize information from your searches and even create a bibliography for you using the documentation style you choose. If you're interested in using one of these programs, first check to see whether your university library has purchased such a program for patron use; if so, it will be available on the library's website, usually with an online tutorial that explains how to use it. Some common reference management software programs are EndNote, Reference Manager, ProCite & RefWorks. If your library does not already make one of these commercial programs available on its website, you can find similar software that can be downloaded free by searching online for "reference management software." In addition to compiling your bibliography, many of these programs can also help you to track your searches (much like the search log recommended earlier) and allow you to organize the information you retrieve into folders. However, even if you are using reference management software to compile your bibliography, you will still need an MLA or APA style book to know how to refer to sources within the body of your text.

For Writing and Discussion

1. Locate brief overviews of the MLA and APA citation formats for books and for journal articles, such as those available online at Purdue University's Online Writing Lab, located at http:// owl.english.purdue.edu. What differences between MLA and APA style do you notice in the citation format for books? What differences between the styles exist in the citation format for journal articles?

2. What documentation style will you use for your current bibliographic project? Using the appropriate style manual, locate one example of each type of citation you may need for your project: a book by a single author, a book by two or more authors, an essay in an edited collection, a journal article, a website, and any other type of publication you expect to cite. What is most unusual or unexpected in the citation format of each type of pub-

lication? What additional questions, if any, do you have about citation format?

3. Does your academic library offer a reference management software program on its website? After a preliminary examination of its tutorial, what advantages do you think this program may offer over formatting your own bibliographic citations? What disadvantages, if any, exist for students using this program? Will you use it for your bibliographic research project?

Now that you have gained some strategies and made some initial decisions regarding your bibliographic research, the next chapter will discuss in greater depth the major databases and bibliographies that are most useful for locating scholarly publications about an issue in composition studies.

Works Cited

American Psychological Association. *Publication Manual of the American Psychological Association.* 6th ed. Washington, DC: American Psychological Association, 2010.

Babin, Edith H., and Kimberly Harrison. *Contemporary Composition Studies: A Guide to Theorists and Terms.* Westport, CT: Greenwood P, 1999.

Gelfand, Harold, and Charles J. Walker. *Mastering APA Style: Student's Workbook and Training Guide.* 6th ed. Washington, DC: American Psychological Association, 2010.

Gibaldi, Joseph. *MLA Handbook for Writers of Research Papers.* 7th ed. New York: Modern Language Association of America, 2009.

—. *MLA Style Manual and Guide to Scholarly Publishing.* 3rd ed. New York: Modern Language Association of America, 2008.

Heilker, Paul, and Peter Vandenberg. *Keywords in Composition Studies.* Portsmouth, NH: Boynton/Cook, 1996.

For Further Reading

Badke, William B. *Research Strategies: Finding Your Way Through the Information Fog.* 2nd ed. New York: iUniverse, Inc., 2004.

Bell, Suzanne S. *Librarian's Guide to Online Searching.* Westport, CT: Libraries Unlimited, 2006.

—. "Tools Every Searcher Should Know and Use." *Online* 31.5 (2007): 22–25.

Ojala, Marydee. "Finding and Using the Magic Words: Keywords, Thesauri, and Free Text Search." *Online* 31.4 (2007): 40–42.

Taylor, Terry, Joan Arth, Amy Solomon, and Naomi Williamson. *100% Information Literacy Success.* Clifton Park, NY: Thomson Delmar Learning, 2007.

5 Your Hosts for the Parlor Conversation: Major Databases and Bibliographies in Composition Studies

In this chapter, you will learn about databases and bibliographies that are helpful when researching topics in composition studies. To be an effective researcher, you need to be knowledgeable about multiple databases and bibliographies because each has distinct advantages and disadvantages. Some are more exhaustive in their coverage, while others are more selective and are helpful when you need to identify the sources that are considered essential scholarship on a particular topic. Different databases index different sources (for example, only certain types of publication or only particular journals), and they index these sources differently (for example, using keywords assigned by a bibliographer or keywords contained in an author's annotation or even a scan of all words in the full text). As a result, searching the same keywords in different databases can often yield different results. Even when databases do identify the same source, the information provided about that source can vary widely. Some databases provide a citation only, while others provide an abstract, and the most helpful provide an electronic copy of the full text.

Because of such differences, a single bibliographic resource rarely works well for all tasks; you are better equipped if you have multiple databases and bibliographies at your disposal and understand how and when to use each. Thus, this chapter begins with a detailed explanation of five major databases that are essential to bibliographic research in composition studies. These are the five databases you will consult most: CompPile, WorldCat, MLA, ERIC, and JSTOR. If possible, read this chapter near a computer with internet access so that you can explore these databases as you read about them. The writing and discussion prompts in this chapter will help you to become better acquainted with each database, while also guiding you in identifying sources that discuss your research interest.

This chapter concludes with descriptions of some more minor databases and bibliographies that you may sometimes wish to consult; their usefulness will depend upon the nature of your research topic and the scope of your project. Even if some seem irrelevant to your current research endeavors, they may be useful in your future research endeavors.

FIVE DATABASES ESSENTIAL TO COMPOSITION STUDIES

CompPile

CompPile is located at http://comppile.org and is widely considered to be the best database for locating scholarship in composition studies. Of the five major databases discussed in this chapter, it is the only one that indexes scholarship related to composition studies exclusively. It is further unique because it is a database without subscription fees or any funding source, maintained exclusively by volunteers. It was created in May 2001 by two professors who are committed to making bibliographic resources in composition studies available to everyone, regardless of university affiliation, at no cost. Richard Haswell served as the site's original bibliographer, and Glenn Blalock is the site's webmaster; both remain the site's primary contributors. Lee Honeycutt also facilitated the start of the database by donating his extensive online bibliographic records. The original plan for the database was that it would index all sources related to composition studies published during the years 1939–1999, but in 2007, Haswell and Blalock decided to extend CompPile's coverage to the present. The database is now sustained by faculty and students in composition studies who volunteer to adopt journals to index and by CompPile Associates, unpaid specialists who coordinate the records for a particular scholarly area of the discipline.

Although its homepage describes CompPile as "an inventory of publications in post-secondary composition, rhetoric, technical writing, ESL, and discourse studies," the scope of the database is elsewhere defined more broadly: "study of the ways that writing in English is taught, learned, and practiced after high-school in and out of college" ("Volunteer Guide"). The types of publications indexed are books (including edited collections), journals (including articles, editorials, comment and response pieces, review essays, and special features), and dissertations. The database is comprehensive rather than selective; in August 2009, it included 96,552 records, a huge number given that all are sources related to composition studies.

The default search page in CompPile is designed for an advanced search, with multiple fields offered (e.g., author, title, date, book, journal, pages, search term, annotation) and with Boolean operators identified in a drop-down list for each field. Because CompPile is indexed using a controlled vocabulary, before searching you should consult the glossary on the site to identify the appropriate search term(s) for your topic. Some words that you might find helpful when searching in a multi-disciplinary database are not used as search terms in CompPile because the terms are too common (such as teacher or writing) or may have multiple meanings (such as class or subject). For such words, the glossary identifies alternate keywords. Also, because CompPile's search engine is sensitive to punctuation, hyphenation is often critical; for example, the search term "research report" generates no hits but typing "research-report" yields multiple pages of bibliographic records. By consulting the database's online glossary before a search, you can be assured that you will know which keywords to search to find all the sources in CompPile that are relevant to your research interest.

In CompPile, the results of any search are organized according to publication date, with the most recent sources appearing first; sources published within the same year are alphabetized by author. You can print or export only the records you want by checking a box next to each entry and then clicking the appropriate command near the top of each page. The vast majority of records in CompPile are bibliographic citations only, although if an annotation is available it will appear on the search screen with the record. You can also search for annotations by entering a search term in the annotations field on the search page. Full texts are rarely available, but if an article is published in an open access journal or on a professional organization's website, a direct link to the full text is provided.

In addition to its usefulness in searching for bibliographic records, CompPile provides a companion wiki site called CompFAQs that may be beneficial to your research. CompFAQs began in 2005 and is accessible through the CompPile homepage. Glenn Blalock describes the purpose of the site as follows: "CompFAQs is a wiki site, meant to be a space for collaborating on answers to questions we pose regularly as writing teachers and as administrators of writing programs. CompFAQs provides research-based answers to frequently asked questions; shares solutions to oft-appearing problems; enables the sharing of resources that address common needs" (CompFAQs site). The site lists numerous category headings (e.g., program design, basic writing, assessment, placement, plagiarism), which are used to organize the array of information that users post on this wiki. By clicking on any category, you will see questions and answers related to that concern. The CompFAQs homepage also provides links to the websites of other professional organizations that provide resources in composition studies.

In all, CompPile has several distinct advantages that make it the primary database for anyone doing bibliographic research in composition studies. It is the database that most comprehensively indexes sources relevant to the field, so it should be the first database you consult. Because it is available for free on the internet, everyone can access it. Because it is discipline-specific, searches in CompPile are less likely to yield irrelevant search results than searches done in a multidisciplinary database. CompPile is also invaluable because it indexes books, essays in edited collections, journal articles, and dissertations; many databases index primarily just one type of publication.

CompPile does, however, have a few limitations. Because it depends on volunteers to update its records, its coverage may not be consistently current. To determine how extensively any particular journal has been indexed, locate the CompPile page that lists journals alphabetically at http://comppile.org/site/journals2.php and then for any journal title, click the link to view that journal's complete record. This record indicates what years and issues of the journal have been indexed, as well as other information about the status of that journal's indexing in CompPile. Another restriction of CompPile is that it indexes only sources that address writing done after high school, so it is not an appropriate resource for someone whose primary research interest is writing done by children or adolescents. Finally, CompPile provides bibliographic citations but relatively few annotations and very few full-text articles. Thus, while CompPile is the best database for bibliographic research in composition studies, it is not the only database that one should consult. Searches done in other databases can supplement a CompPile search by yielding additional sources, additional annotations (which can make it easier to quickly assess a source's relevance) and additional full text articles online (which is more convenient than needing to locate hard copies). Also, it is always wise to consult more than one database because the methods that databases use to index sources differ, so the results of searches in different databases will differ too. When you search multiple databases, you can have greater confidence that your search for sources has been comprehensive.

For Writing and Discussion

1. At the time this chapter was written, several forthcoming changes to CompPile were announced on CompPile's blog (for example, adding the capacity to tag sources and to save search histories). Explore the CompPile site at http://comppile.org. How has CompPile changed since its description in this chapter was written? How might the changes you have noted benefit the users of CompPile?

2. Explore the glossary of CompPile. What search terms should you use when searching for bibliographic records on your research topic in this database? Next, conduct a search using these terms. How many sources do these searches yield? How helpful do the sources seem to your project?

3. Explore the CompFAQs wiki that can be accessed from the CompPile homepage. Do any of the categories listed here relate to your research topic? If so, what resources are provided in this category and how might they be useful to your bibliographic project?

4. As explained in this chapter, CompPile is unlike any other database because it is entirely dependent on the efforts of volunteers. Students of composition studies are encouraged to contribute to the database too. In a CompPile blog entry dated August 3, 2008, Glenn Blalock suggests many ways that students can help to enhance CompPile: index some volumes of a journal that have not yet been indexed; choose a publisher and update the list of books related to composition studies that have been released by that publisher; index professional websites related to composition studies; refine the search terms used to index sources; write annotations for sources indexed in CompPile; and write reviews of sources indexed in CompPile. Contributing to

the CompPile database can be a useful way for students just beginning to learn about composition studies to contribute to the work and resources of the discipline. Which of Blalock's suggestions for student contributions most appeal to you for an individual or collaborative class project? Will you commit to making this contribution?

WorldCat

If you use your campus library's catalogue to search for books about your research topic, you will be searching only those books in your university's library, which is likely to be only a small portion of the books published on your research topic. A far more helpful catalogue to use when searching for books is WorldCat. WorldCat is an online catalog of over 85 million holdings in thousands of libraries worldwide, including the Library of Congress, making it the most complete catalogue of library holdings in existence. In addition to books, WorldCat also includes the records of other library holdings, such as journals, videos, music CDs, and other items. WorldCat does not, however, include items that would not be individually catalogued in a library; therefore, while journals are included, you cannot use WorldCat to search for individual journal articles. A record for any item in WorldCat will include not only the citation information you will need for your bibliography, but also the names and locations of all the libraries nearest to you that subscribe to WorldCat and own the item. In addition, WorldCat's records for books often provide links to the publisher's description of the book, the book's table of contents, and sometimes even published reviews and excerpts.

WorldCat is maintained by the Online Computer Library Center (commonly referred to by the acronym OCLC), an organization founded in 1967 so that libraries could more readily exchange information and services for their patrons. WorldCat is available as an online database through OCLC member libraries' websites as well as through a public website. If your university's library has a subscription to WorldCat, it is best for you to access WorldCat through your library's website, as part of OCLC's FirstSearch. If your library is not a member of OCLC, you can still search the WorldCat catalogue directly through its internet site, http://worldcat.org/.

Although the bibliographic records available through both means are identical, the search capacities and the results that are produced will differ in minor ways based on how you access the catalogue. Searching WorldCat through a library's subscription is preferable because then the "Advanced Search" option has more features (including additional limits that can make your search more precise), and an "Expert Search" option is offered that is not available on the public site. Also, once you have found a highly useful book, you can use a "Find similar items" command, available only through your library's subscription. You should also be aware that the default settings for how search results are displayed differ based on how WorldCat is accessed. If you search the catalogue through your library, the search results will be ordered according to the number of libraries that own each book, with the book owned by the most libraries displayed first. If you instead search the catalogue using the WorldCat.org site, the book most closely related to your search terms will be displayed first, regardless of the number of libraries that own the book. You will then need to enter your zip code (or if you are not in the U.S., your country) to see which libraries that own the book are closest to you, whereas the proximity of libraries is automatically configured if you access the database through your library's subscription.

Once you have had an opportunity to become familiar with World-Cat, you will learn how to use features that will allow your searches to be more efficient. Using the advanced search option, you can limit your search by setting such options as language, year(s), and type of material. You can also alter how the search results are ranked: by date, by relevance, or by the number of libraries that own the item. Knowing the number of libraries that own a particular book can help you assess a book's impact on the discipline. Keep in mind, though, that the number of libraries that own a book is not always an accurate measure of the book's merit; for example, books published within the last year or two may be owned by fewer libraries than older books simply because librarians have had less time to become aware of recent books and to purchase and catalogue them.

WorldCat offers several distinct benefits for bibliographic research in composition studies. First, you can use WorldCat to identify books that seem relevant to your research topic and then use your library's interlibrary loan service to borrow any books that are not available at your own library. The records in WorldCat are more current than those in CompPile, so WorldCat is the best database for discovering any books on your topic that have been published quite recently.

WorldCat will also allow you to locate library copies of books that are out of print. Another benefit of WorldCat is that once you have identified some authors who have written an article or book about the topic you are researching, you can do an author search of WorldCat to determine whether any of them have published additional books about that topic.

Also, if you need a journal article that is not available online, in your university's library, or through interlibrary loan, you can use WorldCat to identify which libraries closest to you have the journal and volume you need. To locate journal holdings, choose the advanced search screen, enter the journal's title in a search box and identify it as a title field, and then limit the publication type to "Serial Publications." The search results will indicate not only the libraries that subscribe to the journal but also which volumes of the journal each library owns. You can then decide whether it's worth traveling to that library to copy the article.

The chief limitation of WorldCat is that it is not a periodical index. Again, WorldCat consolidates all of the holdings of thousands of libraries, but because libraries do no individually catalogue the articles in journals, neither does WorldCat. Therefore, to thoroughly search for journal articles you must use CompPile and then supplement your search using periodical indexes like MLA, ERIC, and JSTOR, databases that will be discussed next.

For Writing and Discussion

1. Check the list of databases on your university library's website to determine whether you can access WorldCat through your library's subscription or must use the companion site available on the internet at http://worldcat.org. Once you have located the database, compare the basic, advanced, and (only if you have subscription access) expert search pages. How do the search options differ?

2. Search WorldCat using keywords that represent your research topic. Does this database help you to locate any recent books about your topic that you did not find when searching CompPile?

3. Consult Appendix D to identify the journals related to composition studies that are not available at your own university's library. Use WorldCat to identify other libraries near you that own these journals, and record your findings in the appropriate column of this appendix.

4. Notice that the advanced search page for WorldCat allows you to vary the manner in which your search results are ranked. You can select whether the results are arranged by number of libraries (items owned by the greatest number of libraries are displayed first), relevance to your search terms (items with the greatest relevance are displayed first), date (items published most recently are displayed first) or accession number (items catalogued most recently are displayed first). Describe a reason why each of these options for ranking results might be useful to your bibliographic research.

MLA International Bibliography

The *MLA International Bibliography* is produced by the Modern Language Association (MLA) and is commonly regarded as the chief database for locating scholarship about literature. However, in the year 2000, MLA began to index more journals devoted to rhetoric and composition studies in its bibliography. In addition to journal articles, the *MLA International Bibliography* also selectively includes books and dissertations. This is a commercial database that requires a subscription; it is only available through the website of a subscribing library.

As already discussed in chapter four, the *MLA International Bibliography* uses a controlled vocabulary to index records. You can identify which search terms best represent your research topic by consulting the database's thesaurus. If you enter the keywords you are considering in the thesaurus's search box, you will see suggestions for narrowing, rephrasing, or expanding the keywords you might use to conduct your search. Like many other databases, the *MLA International Bibliography* provides both basic and advanced search pages; it also supports the use of Boolean operators (AND, OR, NOT) when searching.

The table provided in Appendix C identifies the many journals related to composition studies that are indexed in *MLA International Bibliography*. Although this is fewer journals than the journals indexed in CompPile, because this is a commercial database that is not dependent on volunteers, it is more consistently current in its indexing. Therefore, if a journal indexed in *MLA International Bibliography* has published an article about your research topic quite recently, you may be more likely to find that article by searching the *MLA International Bibliography* than by searching CompPile.

An additional feature that makes the *MLA International Bibliography* even more useful to composition researchers is the MLA Directory of Periodicals. Not only does this directory provide useful information about each of the journals indexed in the bibliography, but it also allows you to search for a keyword within a single journal that you think may be especially pertinent to your research topic. For example, someone wanting sources about assessing the work of basic writers could use this directory to search the keyword "assessment" in the *Journal of Basic Writing*, as well as to search the keyword phrase "basic writing" in the journal *Assessing Writing*. To use this function, first find the periodical you wish to search alphabetically within the Directory of Periodicals; then click "Search within this periodical" so that the journal's MLA-assigned title abbreviation (TA) is added to the search box in which you enter your keywords; finally, add any keywords you wish to search in that journal. Searches conducted this way can eliminate many irrelevant search results because you will be searching only in composition-related journals. This feature in the *MLA International Bibliography* is especially valuable because many individual journal websites do not have a keyword search capacity. For instance, in the example cited above, the *Journal of Basic Writing* website does not offer a keyword search at the time of this writing, yet because the journal is indexed in the *MLA International Bibliography*, a keyword search of solely this journal can be conducted using the MLA database's Directory of Periodicals. If the Modern Language Association adds more journals related to composition studies to its bibliography, you can also use the Directory of Periodicals to update Appendix C, which lists journals indexed in this database in 2009.

For Writing and Discussion

1. Locate the *MLA International Bibliography* among your university library's databases. Consult the database's thesaurus to determine what keywords best represent your research topic. Do an advanced search of these keywords in the database. Does this search yield any additional sources that are useful to your

research that you did not find using the CompPile database? If so, what does this experience teach you about the value of using multiple databases when doing bibliographic research?

2. Using the table provided in Appendix C, examine the list of journals related to composition studies that are indexed in the *MLA International Bibliography*. How does the list of journals indexed in this database compare to the lists of journals related to composition studies that are indexed in ERIC and in JSTOR, also shown in this same appendix? What does this comparison teach you about the value of the *MLA International Bibliography* for bibliographic research in composition studies?

3. Using the table in Appendix C, choose one journal that is indexed in the *MLA International Bibliography* that seems especially relevant to your research topic. Then locate this journal in the MLA database's Directory of Periodicals and do a search in just this journal of your research topic. Does this search yield any sources that you have not previously identified? How do you think this ability to search keywords in a specific journal might be helpful in your current and future bibliographic research projects?

ERIC

ERIC is the acronym for the Education Resources Information Center, which is a digital library sponsored by the U.S. Department of Education, more specifically, the Institute of Education Sciences. ERIC provides searches of more than a million bibliographic records related to education, primarily journal articles, but also books, technical reports, conference papers, and other education-related materials. ERIC provides abstracts for many sources and sometimes links to full texts. ERIC can be accessed through your university library's website, as well as through the website http://www.eric.ed.gov. If you use the public ERIC website, you can register at no charge for "My ERIC," which allows you to save and re-run past searches. If you instead access ERIC through your library's subscription, ERIC may be hosted by different database providers that allow enhanced features, such as vocabulary mapping to help in your selection of keywords to search (e.g., the database provider Ovid) or additional full-text journals (e.g., the database provider EBSCO).

ERIC does not use a controlled vocabulary for keyword searches; instead, searching any keyword in ERIC will identify only those
sources that contain that exact keyword. To locate a greater number
of relevant sources and to decrease the number of irrelevant sources (sources that might use that keyword but in a different context),
you can search using an ERIC descriptor. ERIC descriptors are single
words and phrases used to index sources in ERIC according to their
general topic, regardless of the keywords used in the source. Thus,
descriptors are controlled vocabulary, but they are generally broader
than the keywords used as controlled vocabulary in other databases.
To see the full array of ERIC descriptors for topics related to composition studies, locate the thesaurus (available as a tab on ERIC's public
website), then browse the category "subjects of instruction" to find the
descriptors that begin with "writing." Click on any of these descriptors
to see a list of broader, narrower, and related terms.

The advanced search page in ERIC offers several options not found
in other databases. One unique feature is the ability to limit the search
results to a particular level of education, either generally (e.g., junior
high school, two year colleges) or quite specifically (e.g., grade 10).
Also, if the results of an advanced search are numerous, the advanced
search page allows you to narrow your results by adding more limits—such as additional keywords, additional descriptors, fewer types
of publication, and/or a narrower range of publication dates—and to
then search again only within your original results, rather than starting over with a new search; select "search within results" after an advanced search to access this feature.

ERIC provides two workspaces for saving your search history
and search results. To temporarily save selected records, click on the
clipboard icon next to each; you can then print, email, or export the
records collected on "My Clipboard." If you register for My ERIC,
available free of charge, you can also save your results in folders and
access them in a later session.

There are several benefits to searching ERIC when doing bibliographic research in composition studies. First, some of the sources that
ERIC indexes are not indexed in other commercial databases. By looking at the table provided in Appendix C you can identify the journals
related to composition studies that are indexed in ERIC but not MLA
or JSTOR. Primarily, they are journals that publish empirical research
in composition studies (e.g., *Research in the Teaching of English*), as well

as journals that focus on business or technical writing. As this table indicates, ERIC indexes some journals comprehensively (meaning that every article in that journal during the dates specified is included) and some journals selectively (meaning that only the articles that relate to education are included in ERIC). Another benefit of ERIC is that it includes many of the papers presented at professional conferences, such as the annual convention of the Conference on College Composition and Communication. These are unpublished papers, but they are often available as full texts in the ERIC database because the writer has granted consent.

The indexing of journals is more current in ERIC than in Comp-Pile; ERIC updates its database twice a week and includes records for sources within a month of ERIC acquiring the source. Yet another benefit of searching ERIC is that because the database indexes sources that discuss education at all levels, from early childhood through higher education, ERIC is the best database for researching publications about writing done prior to college. Recall that CompPile indexes only sources that discuss writing done in and after college.

For Writing and Discussion

1. It is often useful to search both the *MLA International Bibliography* and ERIC databases. Nevertheless, based on the descriptions provided in this chapter, which of these databases seems better suited to your research topic? Why?

2. Register for the free workspace "My ERIC" at http://www.eric. ed.gov. How do you think the ability to save searches into folders here can be helpful to your research? What might be some useful folder names for your project?

3. Consult the ERIC thesaurus. What descriptors are most appropriate for your research topic?

4. Do an advanced search on your research topic using one or two keywords and a descriptor. If this search yields more than twenty sources, use the "search within results" feature to add additional limits and search again. Has this search yielded any sources that are helpful to your research that you did not find in either CompPile or the *MLA International Bibliography?*

JSTOR

JSTOR is an unusual database because it is a searchable archive of many core scholarly journals. In other words, for each journal it indexes, JSTOR provides full texts of all the articles published in that journal, beginning with the journal's first issue, except for issues published recently. JSTOR uses the term "moving wall" to describe which recent issues of a journal are not included in the database. A moving wall of three years, for example, would mean that not including the current partial year, the most recent issue of that journal available in JSTOR is three years old (e.g., in December 2008, the most recent issue in JSTOR would be December 2004; beginning in January 2009, all 2005 issues would become available). In 2009, seven journals that are directly related to composition studies were available in JSTOR: *College Composition and Communication* (moving wall of 3 years), *College English* (moving wall of 3 years), *English Journal* (moving wall of 3 years), *Rhetoric Review* (moving wall of 5 years), *Rhetoric Society Quarterly* (moving wall of 7 years), *Rhetorica* (moving wall of 3 years), and *TESOL Quarterly* (moving wall of 5 years). A full list of additional journals indexed in JSTOR, some of which may impact your research if your topic is multidisciplinary, is available on the database site.

Rather than providing full text in raw form, JSTOR provides digitized, high-resolution images of the original journal pages. This means that unlike electronic full texts retrieved from other databases, it is possible to quote from an article retrieved from JSTOR and cite the exact page number for that citation without needing to consult a hard copy of the original journal issue. JSTOR's terms and conditions allow users to download and store one electronic copy of any article in its database as well as to print one copy for personal, noncommercial use, but not to download an entire issue of a journal or print multiple copies of the same article. Even in the rare cases when these terms might seem to restrict a user's bibliographic work—for example, if a journal has published a special issue that is entirely devoted to one's research topic—JSTOR can still be used to read the articles from the issue online before downloading and printing those that seem most helpful. To download or print any article after viewing it, click on the PDF icon so that the article opens in a PDF reader such as Adobe Reader, a free software program you may already have on your computer or that can be downloaded through JSTOR's help menu. You must use the file menu of your PDF reader rather than your internet browser to save and print articles.

JSTOR provides several unique search options. When using the advanced search page to search for a keyword, you can choose to search just the title or just an abstract or the entire full text. When you search the entire text for a keyword and opt to rank the results by relevance rather than date, JSTOR will list first those sources that use the keyword most often, relative to the length of the article. When selecting multiple keywords, you can even boost the consideration of one keyword over another when assessing relevance by using the caret symbol and any numerical value; for example, the keyword "gender^3" along with the keyword "portfolio" would mean that in this search, the database will consider the appearance of the word gender to be three times as important as the appearance of the word portfolio. Proximity searches of multiple keywords are also easily conducted in JSTOR through its drop-down menu selection; you can select "near 5," "near 10," or "near 25" to search only for sources in which your keywords appear within 5, 10, or 25 words of each other. You can also limit your advanced search to only specific journals or specific disciplines (be sure to select both "Language and Literatures" as well as "Education" if you wish to include all journals related to composition studies). If a search returns too many results, you can choose to search within the results rather than beginning again.

In addition to basic and advanced search pages, JSTOR also offers an "Article Locator" search, which allows you to retrieve the full text of an article by entering its complete or partial citation information. This is particularly helpful if you have identified a source using another database such as CompPile and need only to retrieve a copy of the full text. Remember, though, that this will only work if the article you need is published in one of the journals indexed by JSTOR and if the article was published prior to that journal's "moving wall" so that it is available in this archive.

JSTOR can only be accessed through a library's subscription. If your university's library does not subscribe to JSTOR, you can determine if another library you have access to subscribes by checking the site http://www.jstor.org, which provides a list of all subscribing libraries, including public libraries, under "Current Participants." Once you have accessed JSTOR, it is useful to register for "My JSTOR," a feature that allows you to save citations, email citations, and export citations to bibliographic software.

For Writing and Discussion

1. JSTOR contracts individually with journals to determine the length of the "moving wall" that excludes from the database issues published in recent years. What do you think that JSTOR, which is a not-for-profit organization, and journal publishers are each trying to accomplish by making the full texts of older issues readily available but excluding issues published recently?

2. If your library subscribes to JSTOR, use the advanced search page to simultaneously search at least two keywords related to your research topic. Compare the difference in number and relevancy of results when you search these words by title, by abstract, and by full text. Based on your search results, when might you want to choose each search option? Has the full text search helped you to identify any useful articles that you did not find in other databases?

3. Using the JSTOR advanced search page, compare a search done of at least two keywords with no limit on journals to a search of the same keywords with a limit set to search only the journals in the disciplines of Education and of Language and Literature (selecting these two will include all journals related to composition studies). What does a comparison of these search results teach you about the usefulness of limiting the journals searched?

4. Try a JSTOR advanced search of at least two keywords related to your research topic and choose full text search with a proximity marker for the distance between these words in the text (near 5, near 10, or near 25). Next, search at least two keywords and use the caret symbol to give greater weight to the relevancy of one keyword. Based on your search results, in what situations do you think using these search options might improve your search efforts?

Table 2 summarizes the information presented in this chapter about the five major databases for composition studies. In the remainder of this chapter, additional databases and bibliographies related to composition studies are discussed.

Table 2: Synopsis of Major Databases for Composition Studies

Database	Access	Main Search Features	Advantages of Database
CompPile	http://comppile.org	• Advanced search page • Consult glossary for search terms	• Only database devoted solely to composition studies • Open access • Indexes books, essays in collections, journal articles, dissertations, etc. • Links to companion wiki site CompFAQs
WorldCat	Library subscription (preferred for more features) or http://worldcat.org	• Basic, advanced, and expert search pages	• Most complete catalogue of library holdings • Indexes books, journals, etc. but not journal articles • Best source for finding books
MLA International Bibliography	Library subscription only	• Basic and advanced search pages • Consult thesaurus for search terms • Use "Directory of Periodicals" to search within single journal	• Indexes composition studies books and journals since 2000 • Indexes journals shown in Appendix C
ERIC	Library subscription or http://www.eric.ed.gov	• Basic and advanced search pages • Search any keyword or consult thesaurus for descriptors • Can limit search by grade level	• Indexes sources related to education • Indexes journals shown in Appendix C • Includes full texts of some conference papers
JSTOR	Library subscription only; see www.jstor.org for participating libraries	• Basic and advanced search pages • Search term in title, abstract, or full text • Use Article Locator to find full text of citation	• Provides digital images of journal pages • Allows user to save and print full texts • Indexes journals shown in Appendix C

ADDITIONAL BIBLIOGRAPHIC RESOURCES

Dissertation Indexes

Dissertations are another useful source for bibliographic research, both because dissertations are often a comprehensive discussion of a narrow topic and because most have an extensive bibliography you can use to find additional sources for your own research. Citations for dissertations can be found in CompPile and WorldCat, and citations and abstracts of many dissertations related to composition studies are provided on the WAC Clearinghouse site at http://wac.colostate.edu/theses/. However, the most comprehensive indexes of dissertations are those available through the company ProQuest. One such index is Dissertation Abstracts Online, a subscription database that includes over two million records of dissertations published in North America and Europe since 1861. Abstracts are available in this database for dissertations published since 1980, and thesis abstracts are available since 1988. Dissertation Abstracts Online may be available through your university library's website.

Other ProQuest dissertation indexes are the ProQuest Dissertations and Theses (PQDT) database, which includes nearly two million dissertations in full text format, and printed library guides, including *Dissertations Abstracts International* (DAI), *Masters Abstracts International* (MAI), and *American Doctoral Dissertations* (ADD), which includes nearly all dissertations published in the United States regardless of publisher but provides no annotations. More information about each of these indexes and other services for searching and ordering dissertations is available at the ProQuest website, http://www.il.proquest.com/products_umi/dissertations/individuals.shtml.

Many of these databases provide abstracts of the dissertations. Use these abstracts to judge how relevant a dissertation may be to your project before trying to locate it. Because few copies exist of most dissertations, it can be difficult to locate one you may need through interlibrary loan, and ordering your own copy can be costly.

Journals' Websites

Although periodical indexes can be extremely useful in enabling you to search numerous journals simultaneously, the most recent issues of journals may not yet be included in these cumulative indexes, and some journals relevant to your research interests may not be indexed at all. In these situations, it can be helpful to examine an individual journal's website. Most journals have websites; however, what can be found on a website varies greatly from journal to journal. Some websites offer only a description of the journal and/or the sites are not regularly updated. Others provide archives of past issues, some with tables of contents only, some with abstracts of each article, and some with full texts of the articles available for purchase or provided free of charge. Some journal websites provide a search function to help you identify relevant articles in the journal quickly, whereas others do not. Appendix B provides a brief description of each major journal related to composition studies, including the website address of each journal and the site's features at the time this chapter was written.

The table in Appendix C can help you determine the extent to which you may have already searched for articles in a particular journal using *MLA International Bibliography*, ERIC or JSTOR, so that you do not replicate your efforts. Often, you may need a journal's website only to check whether a journal's recent issues (the last couple years that may not yet be included in an index) include an article pertinent to your research project. Or, if a journal exists that is especially relevant to your research interest (e.g., *Computers and Composition; Journal of Basic Writing, Journal of Second Language Writing, The Writing Center Journal*), it can be useful to examine that journal's website more closely to browse its tables of contents and to see what other resources the journal's website may offer. Furthermore, if you notice that two or more articles you have cited in your bibliography were published in the same volume of the same journal, it's useful to check that volume's table of contents (which can often be done online through the journal's website) to see if that volume is a special issue that might contain additional articles related to your topic.

Other Online Bibliographies

Bibliographies compiled by others can be extremely helpful in directing you to books, journal articles, and other sources about your research topic. The bibliographies described in this section, listed alphabetically, are particularly convenient because they exist online. Consulting these bibliographies can help you to find numerous sources about your research topic quickly. Be aware as you use these, however, that no bibliography can equip you with all of the possible sources relevant to your research. Use these online bibliographies to supplement your bibliographic research efforts, not to replace your own searches.

The Bedford Bibliography for Teachers of Writing. Bedford/St. Martin's Publishers issued the sixth edition of its complimentary bibliography in 2003. It can be accessed online at http://bedfordstmartins.com/bb. The bibliography is not searchable by keyword; instead, sources are listed under major and minor subheadings. The bibliography makes no attempts to be comprehensive, but this is a good source for identifying the core scholarship on topics such as rhetoric history, rhetoric theory, the composing process, literacy, writing skills, assessment, curriculum, and programs. The bibliography also offers a section listing other rhetoric bibliographies, as well as an index for locating sources by author. Substantial annotations are provided for all sources.

Bibliographies on Specific Topics in Composition. Bibliographies on specific subspecialties in composition are readily available online. Links to many of these bibliographies are available at http://rhetoric.eserver.org, including bibliographies on Aristotle's *Rhetoric,* technical communication, gender and the history of rhetoric, and visual rhetoric, among others. In addition, an extensive bibliography on computers and composition is available at the *Computers & Composition* journal's website, http://computersandcomposition.osu.edu/bibliography/a.htm. An annotated bibliography on writing across the curriculum can be found at the WAC Clearinghouse site, http://wac.colostate.edu/bib/. In addition to Bedford/St. Martin's more general bibliography (described above), in 2005 the publisher also released the second edition of *The Bedford Bibliography for Teachers of Basic Writing,* available at http://www.bedfordstmartins.com/basicbib/.

Rebecca Moore Howard, a professor at Syracuse University, has compiled and posted bibliographies for many years on nearly a hundred topics in composition studies. Her initial bibliographies are available at http://wrt-howard.syr.edu/bibs.html. More recently, she keeps bibliographies at http://www.citeulike.org/user/senioritis. Both sites are well worth investigating.

For other online bibliographies about specific topic in composition, consult the "bibliographies" sections of CompPile, located at http://comppile.org/site/compbibs.php, *The Bedford Bibliography for Teach-*

ers of Writing, located at http://www.bedfordstmartins.com/bb/reso2. html, and EServer, located at http://rhetoric.eserver.org.

CCCC Bibliography of Composition and Rhetoric 1984–1999. This is an online compilation of annual print bibliographies for the field that were published prior to the year 2000, when composition scholarship was not yet included in the periodical index *MLA International Bibliography.* The first two volumes were originally published under the title *Longman Bibliography of Composition and Rhetoric* and included scholarly work in composition published in 1984 through 1986. The nine volumes that followed annually were titled *CCCC Bibliography of Composition and Rhetoric* and included scholarly work in composition studies published in 1987 through 1995. The data from all eleven of these volumes was then merged, updated to include composition scholarship through 1999, and is now available at the website http://www.ibiblio.org/cccc.

The site offers both basic and advanced search options. The advanced search options allow you to set various limits on the search, including a "Classification" window that allows you to search for sources that appear in only a particular section of the bibliography. There are 26,760 composition-related sources in the bibliography, including journal articles, books, scholarly essay collections, dissertations, and sources indexed in ERIC. Descriptive (rather than evaluative) annotations are provided for all of the sources, although none of the sources can be retrieved through this site. Again, the sources included span only the years 1984–1999.

EServer. EServer provides two websites that are helpful resources for composition researchers. For online information related to rhetoric, the website http://rhetoric.eserver.org provides glossaries of rhetorical terms, links to weblogs, and other useful resources, but most pertinent for a bibliographic endeavor, there are links to rhetoric bibliographies on specific topics. Another website by this provider, http://tc.eserver. org, provides extensive information about technical communication, including a lengthy list of bibliographies. Both sites offer links to other online resources, rather than providing searches for individual, published sources.

Print Bibliographies

Because some print bibliographies in composition studies are now available online, such as the *CCCC Bibliography of Composition and Rhetoric* (see Hawisher and Selfe; Lindemann; Stygall; Taylor) and the *Bedford Bibliography for Teachers of Writing* (Reynolds et al.), you do not need to consult their print versions. Other print bibliographies exist, however, that are not replicated online, and these may also be worth examining.

Bibliographic Books. By using the WorldCat database, introduced earlier in this chapter, you can find some bibliographic books in composition studies. Even bibliographic books that are quite dated can be helpful in tracing how the treatment of specific topics in composition studies has developed historically. One such book is Gary Tate's *Teaching Composition: Twelve Bibliographical Essays,* published in 1987. Greenwood Press published several bibliographic books in the 1980s and 1990s on such topics as basic writing, collaborative writing, research in composition, word processors and the writing process, and writing centers. Other bibliographies can be found by entering your research topic and "bibliography" in WorldCat advanced search boxes. Alternately, search in WorldCat for a bibliographic book such as the *Teaching Composition* text cited above, and then click on the descriptors at the bottom of that record to locate other bibliographies in composition studies. Remember that bibliographic books will be limited in their coverage to the book's own publication date. Update any bibliographies you find with more recent sources found through other means.

Bibliographic Essays. Just as "bibliography" can be entered as a keyword in WorldCat to find bibliographic books, so too can the keyword "bibliography" be searched in ERIC, MLA, and JSTOR databases, all described earlier in this chapter, in order to find any existing bibliographic essays on your research topic.

You should also be aware that certain journals publish bibliographies routinely. During the years 1967–2003, the journal *Research in the Teaching of English* (*RTE*) published a selective bibliography of research reports in composition studies twice a year, in every May and November issue, and those bibliographies included annotations of the sources beginning in May 1973. In 2004, the bibliography in *RTE* became annual and is published each November, with selected sources annotated and a more extensive list of relevant citations that are not annotated. Also, every issue of *Journal of Second Language Writing* includes a selected bibliography of recent scholarship about the topic of second language writing.

Bibliographies of Previously Located Sources. It should go without saying that one of the best places to search for sources on your topic is to examine the references or works cited pages of any source that you find about your topic. Of course, all the sources contained in such bibliographies will precede the publication date of the source you are consulting, so be aware of the historical context of all bibliographies and perform thorough searches using other databases to find relevant sources published more recently.

For Writing and Discussion

1. Scan the list of journals provided in Appendix B. Are there any journals that seem particularly relevant to your research topic? If so, locate the websites for these journals. Do the websites offer features that help you to identify additional sources for your project that you did not find using a major database?

2. In addition to the CompPile, WorldCat, MLA, ERIC, and JSTOR databases, which of the other resources described in this chapter seem to be promising resources to examine regarding your specific research interest? Why?

3. Are there any resources discussed in this chapter are not helpful for your current research topic, even though you suspect they may be quite helpful for other topics that interest you? Which resources do you most look forward to consulting in the future? Why?

Remember that in addition to the databases and bibliographies discussed in this chapter, there are other databases that can be helpful to consult if your topic is multidisciplinary. There are also other genres of disciplinary knowledge—such as mailing list archives and statements by professional organizations—that are typically not indexed in databases but are also useful to consult. The next (and final) chapter recommends a process for using the databases and other resources discussed here to research your topic. Chapter six also explains how to complete some common bibliographic writing assignments.

WORKS CITED

Adler-Kassner, Linda, and Gregory R. Glau. *The Bedford Bibliography for Teachers of Basic Writing.* 2nd ed. New York, NY: Bedford/St. Martin's, 2005. 20 September 2008 <http://www.bedfordstmartins.com/basicbib/>.

American Doctoral Dissertations. Ann Arbor, MI: University Microfilms International, 1964- .

"Bibliography." *Computers & Composition: An International Journal.* 2008. The Ohio State University. 20 September 2008 <http://computersandcomposition.osu.edu/bibliography/a.htm>.

Dissertation Abstracts Online. ProQuest LLC.

Dissertations Abstracts International. Ann Arbor, MI: University Microfilms, 1938- .

ERIC: Educational Resources Information Center. Institute of Education Sciences. 20 September 2008 <http://www.eric.ed.gov>.

The EServer Technical Communication Library. 2001. EServer. 20 September 2008 <http://tc.eserver.org>.

Haswell, Richard, and Glenn Blalock. CompPile 1939-Current. 20 September 2008 <http://comppile.org>.

—. "Volunteer Guide to Indexing Journals." June 2008. CompPile. 20 September 2008 <http://comppile.org/volunteer/guide/Volunteer_Guide_for_Journals.pdf>.

Hawisher, Gail E., and Cynthia L. Selfe. *CCCC Bibliography of Composition and Rhetoric, 1991.* Carbondale, IL: Southern Illinois UP, 1993.

—. *CCCC Bibliography of Composition and Rhetoric, 1992.* Carbondale, IL: Southern Illinois UP, 1994.

—. *CCCC Bibliography of Composition and Rhetoric, 1993.* Carbondale, IL: Southern Illinois UP, 1995.

—. *CCCC Bibliography of Composition and Rhetoric, 1994.* Carbondale, IL: Southern Illinois UP, 1996.

Howard, Rebecca Moore. *Bibliographies for Composition and Rhetoric.* Syracuse University. 20 September 2008 <http://wrt-howard.syr.edu/bibs.html>.

—. CiteULike: Senioritis' Library. 20 September 2008 <http://www.citeulike.org/user/senioritis>.

Jory, Justin, ed. *The WAC Clearinghouse Bibliography.* Colorado State University. 20 September 2008 <http://wac.colostate.edu/bib/>.

JSTOR. 2000. 20 September 2008 <http://www.jstor.org>.

Lindemann, Erika. *CCCC Bibliography of Composition and Rhetoric, 1987.* Carbondale, IL: Southern Illinois UP, 1990.

—. *CCCC Bibliography of Composition and Rhetoric, 1988.* Carbondale, IL: Southern Illinois UP, 1991.

—. *CCCC Bibliography of Composition and Rhetoric, 1989.* Carbondale, IL: Southern Illinois UP, 1991.

—. *CCCC Bibliography of Composition and Rhetoric, 1990.* Carbondale, IL: Southern Illinois UP, 1992.

—. *Longman Bibliography of Composition and Rhetoric, 1984–1985.* White Plains, NY: Longman, 1987.

—. *Longman Bibliography of Composition and Rhetoric, 1986.* White Plains, NY: Longman, 1988.

Masters Abstracts International. Ann Arbor, MI: University Microfilms International, 1986- .

MLA International Bibliography. MLA Office of Bibliographic Information Services.

ProQuest Dissertations and Theses Database. 2008. ProQuest LLC. 20 September 2008 <http://www.il.proquest.com/products_pq/descriptions/pqdt.shtml>.

Reynolds, Nedra, Bruce Herzberg and Patricia Bizzell. *The Bedford Bibliography for Teachers of Writing.* 6th edition. New York, NY: Bedford/St. Martin's, 2003. 20 September 2008 <http://www.bedfordstmartins.com/bb>.

Rhetoric and Composition. 13 February 2007. EServer. September 20, 2008 <http://rhetoric.eserver.org>.

Stygall, Gail. *CCCC Bibliography of Composition and Rhetoric, 1995.* Carbondale, IL: Southern Illinois UP, 1999.

Tate, Gary. *Teaching Composition: Twelve Bibliographical Essays.* Fort Worth: Texas Christian UP, 1987.

Taylor, Todd, ed. *The CCCC Bibliography of Composition and Rhetoric, 1984–1999.* 2002. National Council of Teachers of English. 20 September 2008 <http://www.ibiblio.org/cccc>.

WorldCat. 2001. OCLC Online Computer Library Center, Inc. 20 September 2008 <http://worldcat.org>.

6 Synthesizing the Parlor Conversation: Completing Bibliographic Assignments in Composition Studies

Because so many bibliographic resources and strategies have been discussed in this book, you may feel uncertain about your ability to consolidate the advice from previous chapters to complete a major bibliographic assignment. This chapter offers support by recommending a process for researching and composing two common bibliographic assignments in composition studies: an annotated bibliography and a literature review. The advice offered here relies upon what you have learned in earlier chapters—the modes of inquiry and the genres of publication that are common in composition studies (chapters 2 and 3), the decisions to make when preparing for bibliographic research (chapter 4), and the major databases and bibliographic resources in composition studies (chapter 5)—while offering additional suggestions for making the process of researching and writing bibliographic assignments both thorough and expedient.

Professors have several reasons for requiring bibliographic projects. First, these assignments expose you to the range and depth of scholarly publications in composition studies, so they are a useful way of introducing you to the discipline. They also increase your knowledge about the specific topic you are researching, informing you about what is already known so that you do not merely replicate previous scholarship. Also, because reading much of what has been written about the topic you are researching allows you to articulate probing questions that build upon others' work, bibliographic assignments prepare you to contribute to the existing knowledge about composition studies. Once again, if scholarly publications in a discipline can be construed as a conversation taking place in a parlor, a bibliographic assignment provides an opportunity for you to synthesize what has already been said and to prepare for your own contribution to that conversation.

THE BIBLIOGRAPHIC SEARCH PROCESS

The initial steps in the bibliographic search process are the same, regardless of whether you are writing an annotated bibliography or a literature review. What follows are suggestions for identifying your citations, evaluating and refining your working bibliography, and obtaining hard copies of your sources.

Identifying Your Citations

After you have defined your research topic, identified your search terms, and chosen a documentation format, using the guidelines in chapter four, you are ready to begin looking for sources. There are several reasons why it is wise to begin your bibliographic search by looking first for books. In addition to making you more knowledgeable about your topic, books will aid your later bibliographic searches by helping you identify specialists in your area of interest, helping you expand the keywords you may want to use for your searches, and leading you to additional sources through the books' extensive bibliographies. Yet another reason to search for books first is because books that are not owned by your university's library and that you must request through interlibrary loan may take some time to arrive. If you submit your interlibrary loan requests early in your bibliographic search for sources, you can use the time that it takes for the books to arrive to search for journal articles and other types of sources.

To search for books, use the keywords you identified for your research interest to search the WorldCat database, described in chapter five. Recall that if your university's library subscribes to WorldCat, you can use more features of the database if you access the database through your library's website; otherwise, you can use the public domain version of the database at http://worldcat.org/. Make use of any information offered about the books you locate—such as the publisher's description, table of contents, or reviews—to determine which books from your searches will be useful for your bibliography. Record the citations for these books in your bibliography, and if any of the books seem exceptionally pertinent to your research interests, search for published reviews of that book as well.

Although it may seem easiest to find all of your citations first and then make just one trip to the library to retrieve your sources, you can vastly improve your searches of other databases if you instead pause first to investigate some of the initial books you have found. Borrow those that are owned by your library and complete interlibrary loan requests for the books your library does not own so that they can be delivered soon. How does skimming several of the books you have found improve your understanding of your research topic, particularly in terms of what the discipline may already know about your topic? What keywords do the books use to describe your research interests that you have overlooked in your own list of potential keywords? Which authors seem to be specialists on your topic that you should search as authors to find additional sources? Add these new keywords and authors to a log of searches you plan to conduct in various databases (see chapter four for a search log template).

The next database you should consult is CompPile, the primary database for composition studies, which includes books, journal articles, and other publication formats, available at http://comppile.org. As explained in chapter five, use the glossary feature of the database to ensure that you are using the best search terms for your topic. Recall that the sources in CompPile are organized according to their publication dates, with the most recently published sources listed first. Because CompPile is a discipline-specific database designed exclusively to meet the needs of students and professionals in composition studies, searching CompPile is likely to be your most productive search, yielding the greatest number of relevant sources and the least number of irrelevant ones. Export the citations that seem useful to add to your bibliography. While you have the CompPile database open, also check the CompFAQs wiki link on the homepage to see if any information there is relevant to your topic.

Because databases index different sources and often use different keywords even when they index the same sources, next you should supplement the bibliography you have generated using WorldCat and CompPile by searching your topic in the remaining major databases in composition studies that were discussed in chapter five: the *MLA International Bibliography,* ERIC, and JSTOR. Make use of the titles and any online abstracts to determine which sources meet your search criteria and should be included in your bibliography. For those sources, record the citation information and save all of the information that can help you with your annotations and literature review. Online annotations can be copied and pasted under each citation into your notes to provide a handy synopsis of each source, although you will later need to write original annotations that are your own work and that better summarize and evaluate each source in relation to your bibliographic project. When full texts of the articles are available in a database, print them for your later reading.

Once you have retrieved the majority of book and journal article citations for your bibliographic assignment through these major databases, there are several additional bibliographic resources you should consult. Chapter five of this book identifies additional online and print bibliographies; those listed under the heading "Bibliographies on Specific Topics in Composition" may be especially useful. Also, even though dissertations can be very difficult to obtain, you may still wish to use one of the dissertation indexes discussed in chapter five to determine whether a dissertation has been published that is closely related to your research interest; if so, add its citation to the draft of your bibliography and determine later whether the dissertation seems so useful to your project that it's worth the effort to locate it. Perhaps most importantly, if the topic you are researching is interdisciplinary, you should also consult the descriptions of databases on your library's website in order to identify additional databases that may be helpful in locating relevant sources. A reference librarian can also assist you in choosing the databases best suited for specific disciplines other than composition studies.

Once you have concluded your search of databases and bibliographies, scan the list of journals identified in Appendix B to identify any journals that might be especially pertinent to your research interests. When you have identified the journals you should consult further, use Appendix C to determine the extent to which you have already searched these journals using the *MLA International Bibliography*, ERIC, and JSTOR databases. You can also determine the extent to which you have searched the journal in CompPile by referring to the CompPile page that lists journals alphabetically, located at http://comppile.org/site/journals2.php; click the far right column to view the complete record of any journal title, which indicates the years and issues of the journal that have been indexed in CompPile. After you confirm how thoroughly you have already searched a particular journal using databases, you will know the extent to which you should search that journal further using the journal's website or an alternate database that is recommended for the journal in Appendix B. It may be that you will need to search the journal's website for only the most recent issues that may not yet be indexed.

Next, investigate whether any professional organization related to composition studies offers resources that pertain to your research interest. There are links to the websites of professional organizations on the CompPile homepage, and as discussed in chapter four, you can often find on these websites position statements and other professional resources. Be especially careful to transcribe the web address of any online source that opens as a PDF document (for example, a text that requires Adobe Acrobat) because the address will not print on the document, making the source hard to relocate.

By now you should have citations for your bibliography that represent many of the publication genres that are vital to the dissemination of knowledge in composition studies—books, essays in edited collections, journal articles, dissertations, professional organizations' website resources and position statements—but your citations may not as fully represent the modes of inquiry used to construct knowledge in composition studies: scholarship, empirical research, and practice. If nearly all of the citations you have found are scholarship (theory, history, and criticism), deliberately search for additional citations of empirical research about your topic. To do this, search your topic in CompPile and add "data" as an additional search term. Also, do an advanced search of your topic in the ERIC database and add *Research in the Teaching of English* as a search limit because this is a journal that publishes many research reports related to composition studies. Also, search for sources about your topic in *Written Communication,* a journal which also publishes many research reports but that is not indexed in the *MLA International Bibliography,* ERIC, or JSTOR; you can search *Written Communication* using the Sage website that is identified for the journal in Appendix B. Dissertations are another common genre for empirical research reports, so you may also want to return to the suggestions already provided for locating dissertations about your topic.

Although citations to knowledge manifested as practice should not comprise the majority of your bibliography (except perhaps in rare situations, with the prior approval of your professor), the inclusion of a few citations that represent practice may be appropriate. If you determine that disciplinary practice plays a significant role in knowledge about your topic, you can look for relevant examples in composition textbooks, on department websites, and on blogs. A general search engine like Google or Yahoo can lead you to some sources of disciplinary practice; just be certain to discuss such sources in your bibliographic assignments in ways that clearly acknowledge these sources as nonscholarly. You can also search for knowledge based on practice in the archives of mailing lists related to composition studies. Recall, as explained in chapter four, that mailing lists are not formally indexed, so you will need to experiment with your search terms to find the terms that contributors may have used when they posted about your topic.

Although the process of finding citations that has been described here seems linear, in actuality, it is recursive. The more sources you find, the more you will learn about your topic and the more likely you are to conceive of your topic differently. As your understanding of your topic grows, you will be better able to refine your topic and identify new search terms. You may often, then, need to return to databases and other resources you have used previously to search again for these new terms.

Evaluating and Refining Your Bibliography Draft

It can be difficult to decide when to stop searching for sources. If you are completing a bibliographic assignment for a course, your professor may require a minimum number of sources for the assignment. However, you should not necessarily stop searching just because you have found the required number of citations. Finding more sources than is required will allow you to later discard the sources that prove to be less relevant than you expected or that add little beyond what is already said in other sources. Also, particularly if you are researching a topic about which you have limited prior knowledge, you may need to read more than you cite in order to ensure that you've fully understood the discipline's current knowledge about your topic. Therefore, search for roughly one-third more than the number of sources you need. If your professor has not required a certain minimum number of sources, decide how many sources you need based on the complexity of your topic and the scope of your assignment, and then increase that estimate by roughly one-third.

After you have gathered one-third more than the number of sources you expect to need, evaluate those sources to determine whether more searching is necessary. Begin by recalling the criteria you developed for your bibliography while reading chapter four. Are all of the sources you have found relevant to your research topic? Are they all sources that readers in composition studies would consider credible? Have you found both recent publications as well as older, core scholarly sources on your topic? Also consider both the depth and range of scholarship that is represented by your bibliography. Will the sources you have found allow you to produce a bibliographic project that is comprehensive? Considered cumulatively, do the sources provide adequate information on all of the subtopics that comprise your research interest? When these criteria are met, and if your next several search attempts yield no useful additions to your bibliography, you may be ready to stop searching.

Before beginning to gather hard copies of your sources, finalize any corrections to your bibliography. Title your bibliography, making sure that all of the subtopics you searched are represented in its title. Ensure that the sources are listed alphabetically according to the first word of the citation (usually the author's last name but when an author's name is not available, the first word of the title). Check that the citation is complete and correctly formatted for each entry. Also make sure that each citation provides the optimal reference for the scholarship you need. That is, if you notice similar sources by the same author, opt for the journal article rather than the conference paper, and the book rather than the article. If you have cited an edited collection but intend to use only selected essays, cite those essays separately, rather than listing the book as a single entry. If you have found an older source reprinted in a more recent collection, consider citing the original publication so that the source's historical context is clearer, unless only the later reprinting is readily available.

For Writing and Discussion

1. Once you have compiled a draft of a bibliography about your research topic, return to the list of criteria that you developed while reading chapter four. Examine your bibliography in light of the earlier decisions you made about each of these criteria: quantity of sources, credibility of sources, relevance of sources, timeliness of sources, and cumulative merit of sources (range of

modes of inquiry and types of publication, length of sources, proportion of sources for each subtopic). In what ways does your bibliography need improvement?

2. Search for additional citations that address the inadequacies of your working bibliography that you have just identified in the prompt above. Once you have added these, have your working bibliography critiqued by classmates and/or your professor so that you will learn other ways in which your selection of sources can be improved. Then search for more sources accordingly.

Obtaining Hard Copies of Your Sources

It is unlikely that you will be able to obtain copies of all the sources cited in your bibliography from your own university's library. As discussed in chapter four, your library's holdings in composition studies will depend upon several factors: the existence of graduate programs related to composition studies at your institution, how long the program has existed (which affects when journal subscriptions may have begun) and its enrollment size, as well as the budget for developing the library collection, how informed the library staff member responsible for humanities orders is about the research needs of students and faculty in composition studies, and how actively the composition studies faculty at your institution request library purchases. If you have answered the questions in Appendix A to assess your university library's holdings in composition studies, you will be able to estimate the extent to which you will need to gather your sources from other libraries.

Even though you have already obtained copies of some books you found using the WorldCat database, you probably found additional books about your topic while searching other databases. Begin, then, by checking your own library's catalogue to see which books in your bibliography are both owned by your library and are currently available. Most libraries now indicate in their online catalog whether the book is currently on the shelf or is already checked out (some even indicate when a borrowed book is due to be returned). You have several options for obtaining books that are not available at your university's library. The easiest option is to request the book through your library's interlibrary loan service. Interlibrary loan requests can often be done online, even when the library is closed; make your requests as soon as possible because it will take time for the books to arrive.

If you are fortunate enough to live within easy traveling distance of another institution that has a graduate program related to composition studies, particularly if it is an institution that has reciprocal borrowing privileges with your own university, you may want to check that university's online library catalog to determine which books not available at your own library are available there. If multiple books are available there, and especially if you discover that the same library also has several of the journal articles that are not available at your own library and that you are not able to locate online, it may be worth traveling to that library to obtain several of the sources you need for your research. Before you go, be sure to confirm what identification will be required of you from that library; it may be simply your student ID card from your own institution, but some also require a letter from your library. If you cannot find this information on the website of your own library or the website of the library you are visiting, phone first.

A final option for obtaining an especially pertinent book is to purchase it yourself. Though this is not a desirable choice for students on frugal budgets, in rare cases it may be your only means of locating a copy of a book that has been published very recently or that is not widely available. A book can be purchased online directly from the publisher; if you are ordering multiple books by different publishers, you can save on shipping costs by ordering from a single distributor like Amazon.com. You may also be able to reduce your expenses by locating a used copy through a site like half.com or Amazon.

Once you have taken the steps necessary to obtain the books you need, you should next focus on obtaining journal articles. Journals may not be checked out from libraries, so even if your library owns many of the issues you need, it is often easier to print copies of full text articles that are available online rather than to locate and photocopy the articles from bound volumes in the library. Because the JSTOR database provides digital page images of all the articles in its database, this database is an excellent source to begin collecting hard copies of the articles in your bibliography. Check Appendix C to determine which of the articles in your bibliography are available in JSTOR, keeping in mind that JSTOR is an archival database, so articles more recent than the "moving wall" designated for each journal will not yet be included. Appendix C indicates only the journals related to composition studies that are currently indexed in JSTOR; if your bibliography contains articles from any major journals in other disciplines, consult the JSTOR database to determine whether those journals are included in JSTOR (at the time of this writing, a list of all journals in the database can be found by following the links from the homepage to "About JSTOR" and then "The Archives" and finally "Journals"). When you are looking for the full text of a particular article in JSTOR, use the "Article Locator" search option to obtain it most easily.

If your library owns the issues you need of other journals not in JSTOR, go to the library to photocopy those articles. Even if electronic copies can be found of these articles, it is unlikely that the online versions would retain the original pagination, which is vital when quoting a passage. Also, simply photocopying articles that are available on your campus is probably more time efficient than trying to locate online versions of numerous articles.

There are several possible means of obtaining articles that are not in JSTOR and that are not owned by your university's library. To attempt to find such an article online, locate the journal's website to see if the article is available for viewing. Some journal websites make articles available free of charge online, particularly if the articles are not recent; others allow you to download articles for a very nominal charge (for example, at the time of this writing, articles published in the journal *Reflections* can be downloaded from the journal's website for $1 per article); other journals contract with a provider who charges a substantial fee for each article (for example, several composition studies journals contract with ScienceDirect, which provides abstracts of all articles but at the time of this writing charges non-subscribers $31.50 per article for full text, regardless of whether the text is a one-page editorial or a forty-page research report). There are also journals that allow individual subscribers to view all past issues of the journal online, so if you need numerous articles from the same journal, you might consider purchasing a one-year subscription to gain online access to them all.

Still another means of obtaining online access to journal articles is to identify all of the databases in which a particular journal is indexed because some of those databases may provide full text copies of articles, even if other databases do not. The descriptions in Appendix B indicate some of the alternate databases for some journals. If you would like to identify all of the databases that index a particular journal, consult *Ulrich's Periodicals Directory*. Your library may subscribe to an online version of this database that it offers through its website like other databases. If you cannot locate an online version of the database, ask a reference librarian for a bound volume that is usually kept at the reference desk. Using *Ulrich's Periodicals Directory*, you can look up any journal alphabetically by its title, and once you have located the full record for that journal, you will see a list of all of the databases that index the journal, including the dates of the journal available in each database (in the online version of *Ulrich's Periodicals Directory*, after locating the journal's record, click on the tab labeled "Abstracting/Indexing & Article Access"). Then, check your library's website again to determine which of these databases your library subscribes to and which might provide full texts of the articles in that journal. When you access one of these databases to look for the full text of a particular article, use the advanced search option, identifying the author, title, journal name, and publication date, so that you can retrieve the article quickly.

For articles you cannot readily obtain online or at your own university's library, use the WorldCat database to determine if another library near you subscribes to the journal and owns the issue you need. If a particular library owns one or more articles that you think are vital to your project, consider traveling there to photocopy them, again ensuring first that you have the identification needed to be permitted access to the library. Before traveling, also ensure that you have organized your list of all the sources you may need from that library so that you need to make only one trip.

If there is no library nearby that owns the journal issues you need, investigate whether you are able to request a copy of an article through your library's interlibrary loan service. Because these services are less common than interlibrary loans for books, you should confirm with a reference librarian at your university the likelihood that this request will be filled and the length of time it may take to do so.

After you have gathered hard copies of your sources, examine the references or works cited pages of the sources to see if they include any pertinent sources you have not found in your own searches. Even if you have been extremely thorough in your own searches, other writers may have a different perspective on your topic and may have used different search terms to locate sources. Therefore, gleaning sources from others' research can make your own bibliography more comprehensive. Older sources about your topic that appear in multiple recent publications are likely to have historic significance and should be added to your bibliography.

For Writing and Discussion

1. Print a copy of your working bibliography. Consult your university library's catalogue, databases that provide full text articles online, and the interlibrary loan services of your library to determine where you can obtain a copy of each source. In the margin of your printed copy, jot the call numbers you will need to retrieve sources that your library owns. For sources that your library does not own and that you cannot retrieve online, complete an interlibrary loan request and record the date of your request next to the citation on your printed copy.

2. What books did you identify as important to your research that were not owned by your own university's library? Are any of these books that you think would be useful to future students in the course or program in which you are enrolled? If so, provide these citations to your professor and ask that he or she request that the books be purchased for your university's library collection. Although the orders are not likely to be completed in time for your own project, future students in composition studies courses at your university will appreciate your help in ensuring that your library's holdings in composition studies are well developed.

WRITING BIBLIOGRAPHIC ASSIGNMENTS

Writing an Annotated Bibliography

An annotated bibliography is simply a bibliography that has, under each citation, a brief summary and evaluation of the source being cited. You may be required to write an annotated bibliography for a course assignment; however, even if it is not a required assignment, writing an annotated bibliography can be useful in preparing you to write a literature review, another common bibliographic assignment.

The first step in writing any annotation is to read the source you wish to annotate. You may wonder, though, whether it's necessary to read each source in its entirety before writing its annotation. Often doing so is unrealistic, especially if many of your sources are books and you have limited time before your annotated bibliography assignment is due. The care you take in reading, then, should be negotiated to satisfy multiple goals: the need to write annotations that summarize the sources accurately, the need to distinguish sources from each other and write annotations that identify the unique contribution each source makes to the discipline's knowledge about your topic; the need to increase your own knowledge so that you can articulate your own position on the topic in a future assignment; and the need to complete your annotated bibliography by the assignment's due date.

If you have copied some annotations or abstracts from databases as you collected citations, it's imperative that you use these only for your own orientation to the source and do not include them verbatim in your assignment. Not only is writing your own annotations an ethical necessity for avoiding plagiarism, but also it is through the process of composing annotations that you best understand a source. Furthermore, an annotation you find elsewhere is not likely to have the appropriate emphasis because annotations in your bibliography should be written to highlight each source's relevance to your specific research interest.

Your goal for each annotation should be to provide a succinct and yet substantive summary of the source as it pertains to your topic. In other words, the annotation need not be an accurate synopsis of the entire source, only of the portion of the source that relates to your research topic. This summary should be several sentences long and should provide a more specific synopsis than could be deduced from the source's title alone. Strive to be both concise and specific. For example, rather than writing simply that a source "discusses common misconceptions" or "provides new solutions," briefly enumerate what those misconceptions or solutions entail. Similarly, if a source discusses "different methods of assessment," which methods does it discuss? If the same source offers "new forms of response," succinctly paraphrase the nature of those responses. Though brief, the annotations should be informative enough that each source in your bibliography is distinguishable from all other sources on the basis of its annotation alone. In fact, incorporating some cross references into your annotations that highlight the distinctions between similar sources will better prepare you for using the annotated bibliography as the basis for writing a literature review.

The final sentence or two of your annotation should be evaluative. Rather than writing a generic comment like "This source is helpful because it discusses my topic," indicate how the source uniquely contributes to your understanding of the topic you are researching. You might write "The question this source raises for my research project is. . ." or "When planning my project, this source will help me to . . ." You can think of the evaluative statement as your rationale for including the source in your bibliography. Although your evaluations should be analytical, they should not reflect any personal biases. For example, when one student in my course wrote "This source gives me more ammunition to shoot holes in traditionally taught grammar," I reminded him that sources should be studied and then used collectively to inform one's opinion; they should not be used simply as "ammunition" to support opinions one has formed prior to carefully studying all the sources one finds.

James Harner makes some additional suggestions about the sentence style of annotations in *On Compiling an Annotated Bibliography.* He recommends that when composing annotations, writers use historical present tense consistently, avoid passive voice, and choose verbs with care because they have different connotations (e.g., "speculates" is more tentative than "asserts") (27). An appendix in Harner's volume, compiled by Ken Bugajski, offers a list of 225 possible verbs for annotations to help writers avoid the monotony of repeating verbs like "explains" and "discusses." Harner suggests as well that writers reread all their annotations in sequence when they are complete to ensure that the style is consistent but not repetitive.

What follows are four sample annotations, all of them of sources that discuss how to write literature reviews. As you read them, note the ways in which these annotations use summary, evaluation, and cross referencing of sources.

Clark, Irene L. "Writing the Literature Review." *Writing the Successful Thesis and Dissertation: Entering the Conversation.* Upper Saddle River, NJ: Prentice Hall, 2007. 103–24.

This chapter discusses the purpose of literature reviews, strategies for reading and taking notes on sources, and methods for keeping track of many sources. Portions of literature reviews are used to illustrate the advice being offered. Even though this book is written to aid students in any discipline, many of the examples used are from composition studies because that is Clark's own academic specialization. Therefore, this book may be more appropriate for students in composition studies programs than Galvan's and Hart's texts, which are written for students in the social sciences. As a chapter about writing literature reviews rather than a full book, it is a succinct guide for students who need to write a literature review for a course project.

Galvan, Jose L. *Writing Literature Reviews: A Guide for Students of the Social and Behavioral Sciences.* 3rd edition. Glendale, CA: Pyrczak Publishing, 2006.

This book is highly process-oriented in its approach to writing literature reviews, with separate chapters on finding sources, analyzing sources, creating tables to summarize sources, planning an outline, drafting the review, receiving feedback on the draft, and revising the review. Subjects treated more thoroughly here than in other guides are how to evaluate both quantitative and qualitative research reports that a writer might locate for a review and how to ensure that a literature review is coherent by using an overview, subheadings, and transitions. Seven complete literature reviews are included as models. Galvan uses numbered headings for the advice in each chapter, making this text highly accessible and suitable for quick reference.

Hart, Chris. *Doing a Literature Review: A Comprehensive Guide for the Social Sciences.* London: Sage, 2001.

Although this book does include advice on writing a literature review, the vast majority of the text is devoted to methods of analyzing the arguments made in sources and using various graphic organizers to synthesize multiple sources. Particularly helpful is the inclusion of several literature reviews, with Hart's own commentary written alongside in the margin, highlighting the techniques used by writers. This book is best for students who want to improve their skills in evaluating sources. It is more densely written than the texts by Clark, Galvan, and Ridley and requires more concentrated reading.

Ridley, Diana. *The Literature Review: A Step-by-Step Guide for Students.* Sage Study Skills Series. London: Sage, 2008.

This book discusses many of the topics found in other sources about literature reviews: the purposes of literature reviews and strategies for reading, note taking, and structuring the review. The great value of this text lies in its treatment of topics discussed only minimally, if at all, by Clark, Galvan and Hart. These include instruction in using reference management software, an entire chapter on alternate methods for citing sources within the review, a chapter on foregrounding the writer's voice within a literature review, and a chapter on referring to the literature review in later chapters of a dissertation or thesis. Like Clark's text, this book is not restricted to disciplines in the social sciences and is therefore useful for students in all disciplines. The advice offered is practical and is often illustrated through quite brief excerpts from literature reviews.

For Writing and Discussion

1. Discuss the above annotations. Do they summarize the sources sufficiently? Are the distinctions between the sources highlighted? Is there additional information you would want to know about these sources?

2. Write annotations of two or three sources you have found that address a common subtopic or issue. Ensure that your annotations summarize the sources, highlight their distinctions, and evaluate the merit of the sources in the context of your research project. After writing your annotations, seek feedback on them from classmates and perhaps your professor.

Writing a Literature Review

A literature review is a common section in both empirical research reports and in graduate theses and dissertations. Generally, the literature review appears early in these texts, shortly after the opening section that identifies the disciplinary need for the project and the question or problem that the study will attempt to resolve. As a section of these texts, a literature review serves several purposes: it establishes your credibility by proving you are knowledgeable about prior scholarship; it informs readers of your text about the need for your own project; and it prepares you to discuss your conclusions in the context of others' scholarship.

It can be helpful to read several literature reviews before writing your own so that you are familiar with the conventions of this genre. Although sample literature reviews are not included in this book, they are readily available in reports of empirical studies that are published in journals such as *Research in the Teaching of English* or *Written Communication,* in theses or dissertations (often a literature review is the first or second chapter), and in book-length research reports (e.g., Janet Emig's case study *The Composing Processes of Twelfth Graders).*

Even if you are not required to write an annotated bibliography for a course assignment, doing so can be a useful means of preparing to write a literature review. Think of annotations as replacing note cards on your sources. You can describe each source succinctly in an annotation and then use the annotations to identify points of comparison and contrast between the sources, making you much better prepared for the difficult task of organizing a literature review.

One of the major tasks in converting an annotated bibliography into a literature review is deciding how to organize the review's discussion of sources. In an annotated bibliography, the organization is nearly effortless: sources are simply arranged alphabetically and except for perhaps some minor cross-references in the annotations, the sources are discussed autonomously. A literature review, though, is written in consecutive paragraphs like an essay, and because it discusses multiple sources simultaneously, its organization requires more deliberation. An error that some students make when writing their first literature review is to organize the review according to the types of publication, so that all books are discussed together and all articles published in the same journal are discussed together. This is never a satisfactory organization because the purpose of a literature review is to orient readers to the topic being researched, not to highlight various publication genres. Thus, the overall structure for your literature review must be derived from patterns you find in the content of your sources.

A useful way to plan the organization of your review is to print a spare copy of your annotated bibliography and use scissors to cut apart the annotated citations from their original alphabetical order. Then reread the annotations and look for common themes among the sources, including sources that discuss the same issue but disagree in their perspective. Consider using a highlighter to mark key phrases in the annotation or to jot marginal notes that remind you of how each source affirms or contests what's said in other sources. Then sort the annotated citations into piles of related sources accordingly. If one source is highly relevant to more than one group, simply print a second copy of that annotated citation to use when sorting so that it can be placed in more than one pile. Each pile will become a section of your review, perhaps as short as a paragraph or as long as several pages, depending upon how many sources are in each pile and how detailed your discussion will be. After you've placed all the sources you want to review in their appropriate piles, decide the most logical order for discussing these groups of sources, as well as the transitions you might use to move your discussion from one group of sources to the next.

Two effective approaches to structuring a literature review are organizing it by subtopics and organizing it by chronological periods. Organizing the review by subtopics works best if your research topic is multi-faceted because this organization allows you to write a brief, separate review for each aspect of the topic you are researching. You may even want to use subheadings to title the discussion of each subtopic. Reviews that are organized chronologically, tracing the development of knowledge about a topic, are less common because composition studies does not have a long history as an academic specialization. Yet if your topic is one that has been discussed in publications for at least a few decades and if perspectives on the topic have changed substantially over time, you may want to organize your literature review by chronological periods to describe how the scholarship about your topic has developed historically. Clearly, the mode of organization that's best for your literature review will depend upon your research topic and the scholarship you have found.

Once you've planned your organization, start writing the paragraphs that will comprise your review. Begin each paragraph with a strong topic sentence. In shorter literature reviews such as those intended for article-length research reports, the topic sentence of most paragraphs should be a statement that's true of multiple sources and that you can discuss further in the body of the paragraph. The emphasis in most paragraphs should be on synthesizing what's said in several sources, rather than summarizing any single source in as much detail as you have done in your annotations. It's even possible to synthesize several sources in one sentence, identifying the sources only parenthetically at the end of the sentence, as in this example: "Some recommend that students be trained as writing fellows to provide the tutoring that supports writing-across-the-curriculum programs (Haring-Smith, 2000; Soven, 2001; Stoecker et al., 1993)." An entire paragraph or more should be written about an individual source only when that source is exceptionally pertinent to your own project or when the literature review is part of a much longer document, such as a thesis, dissertation, or book-length research report.

Keep readers' needs in mind whenever you refer to a source in your review. Identifying the source by its author, rather than just its title or the title of the journal in which an article was published, will enable readers to quickly locate the source you're discussing in your bibliography at the end of the literature review. When the source has more than two authors, you can cite just the last name of the first author and use "et al." to indicate that the source has additional authors so that your prose is not encumbered by a long list of names (e.g., "Andrews et al. conclude that . . ."). Another need of readers is understanding the timeliness of the sources you discuss. If you are using APA style for your literature review, the dates of the sources will be readily apparent in your review; however, if you are using MLA style, you may want to incorporate specific publication dates or at least general time periods into your sentences when knowing the historical context or contemporaneity of a source enhances readers' understanding of the sources you are reviewing.

Writing a conclusion for your literature review will be easier if you remember the purpose of this genre. In a literature review, it is not customary that you advance your own argument or claim. Instead, the primary purpose of a literature review is to provide evidence that others in the discipline are interested in the questions you will address in your own argument that follows the literature review or the hypotheses you will test in your empirical study. The sources you discuss should also confirm that your research questions have not been previously answered and your hypotheses have not been previously verified. If any of your sources appear to be quite similar to the project you are planning, explain the differences that make your project unique. The literature review does not need to end with a conclusion based on your sources; instead, end your literature review by segueing into the questions or hypotheses that you will investigate in an upcoming project.

For Writing and Discussion

1. Locate a literature review that you can read as a model of this genre. Identify the literature review you have read, and then

describe what you notice about its structure and treatment of sources.

2. Write an outline for organizing your literature review that accommodates all of the sources in your bibliography. Note on the outline which sources you will address in each section, making sure that all of the sources in your bibliography are included in the outline. Seek feedback on your outline from classmates.

3. Write a first draft of your literature review. Next, ask several classmates who are unfamiliar with your sources to read your draft and then report to you what they understand about previously published scholarship about your topic. Are there places where they think your review needs to be made more coherent? Are there places where the relationships between your sources needs to be clarified? What are your classmates' suggestions for clarifying the relationship between prior scholarship and your own proposal for further research and study? Use the feedback you receive to revise your literature review.

Joining the Scholarly Conversation

This book has introduced you to the parlor where the disciplinary conversations in composition studies are taking place. Using bibliographic resources, you can listen to the discipline's ongoing conversation and learn what contributions others have made to the knowledge of the discipline. Ultimately, though, bibliographic research is merely a foundation for joining the disciplinary conversation yourself, for becoming an active contributor to knowledge about composition studies.

Once you enter the composition studies conversation, I hope you'll find, as many others have, that you've been fortunate in your choice of academic specialization. In a 1989 address entitled "Composing Ourselves: Politics, Commitment, and the Teaching of Writing," Andrea Lunsford, then the Chair of the Conference on College Composition and Communication, articulated many of the disciplinary characteristics that make a professional engagement in composition studies so rewarding:

- We are strongly interdisciplinary; we blur disciplinary boxes; we blur genres. . . .

- We are non-hierarchical and exploratory, intensively collaborative. . . .
- We are dialogic, multi-voiced, heteroglossic. Our classroom practices *enact* what others only talk about; they are sites for dialogues and polyphonic choruses.
- We are radically democratic and quick to use new technology to further democratize reading and writing for ourselves and our students.
- We are committed to maintaining the dynamic tension between *praxis* and *theoria,* between the political and the epistemological. . . . (76)

Elsewhere, Lunsford describes several of her early experiences as a novice member of the discipline, someone just entering the parlor. She writes that the graciousness extended to her by other members of the profession felt like an invitation into a community, one that "helped me begin to imagine what a life in the profession of composition studies might become" (4). She sums up her understanding of the discipline by writing that "invitations of a particular kind stand for me as a metonymic representation of the nature of composition studies" (4).

It has been my goal to help you feel similarly, that those engaged in the discipline of composition studies invite you to join our community, first to listen and then to apply your intellect, your wise judgment, and your generous spirit to advancing our scholarly conversation. Welcome.

WORKS CITED

Bugajski, Ken. "Appendix: Annotation Verbs." *On Compiling an Annotated Bibliography.* James L. Harner. New York: Modern Language Association, 2000. 45–48.

Clark, Irene L. *Writing the Successful Thesis and Dissertation: Entering the Conversation.* Upper Saddle River, NJ: Prentice Hall, 2007.

Emig, Janet. *The Composing Processes of Twelfth Graders.* NCTE research report No 13. Urbana, IL: National Council of Teachers of English, 1971.

Galvan, Jose L. *Writing Literature Reviews: A Guide for Students of the Social and Behavioral Sciences.* 3rd edition. Glendale, CA: Pyrczak Publishing, 2006.

Harner, James L. *On Compiling an Annotated Bibliography.* New York: Modern Language Association, 2000.

Hart, Chris. *Doing a Literature Review: A Comprehensive Guide for the Social Sciences.* London: Sage, 2001.

Lunsford, Andrea. "Composing Ourselves: Politics, Commitment, and the Teaching of Writing." *College Composition and Communication* 41 (1990): 71–82.

—. "The Nature of Composition Studies." *Introduction to Composition Studies.* Ed. Erika Lindemann and Gary Tate. New York: Oxford UP, 1991. 3–14.

Ridley, Diana. *The Literature Review: A Step-by-Step Guide for Students.* Sage Study Skills Series. London: Sage, 2008.

For Further Reading

Casanave, Christine Pearson, and Stephanie Vandrick, eds. *Writing for Scholarly Publication: Behind the Scenes in Language Education.* Mahwah, NJ: Lawrence Erlbaum, 2003.

Couture, Barbara, and Thomas Kent, eds. *The Private, the Public, and the Published: Reconciling Private Lives and Public Rhetoric.* Logan, UT: Utah State UP, 2004.

The Dissertation Consortium. "Challenging Tradition: A Conversation about Reimagining the Dissertation in Rhetoric and Composition." *College Composition and Communication* 52 (2001): 441–54.

Fontaine, Sheryl I., and Susan Hunter. *Writing Ourselves into the Story: Unheard Voices From Composition Studies.* Carbondale: Southern Illinois UP, 1993.

Foss, Sonja K., and William Joseph Condon Waters. *Destination Dissertation: A Traveler's Guide to a Done Dissertation.* Lanham: Roman & Littlefield, 2007.

McNabb, Richard. "Making the Gesture: Graduate Student Submissions and the Expectation of Journal Referees." *Composition Studies* 29 (2001): 9–26.

Olson, Gary A., and Todd W. Taylor. *Publishing in Rhetoric and Composition.* Albany: SUNY P, 1997.

Peterson, Patricia Webb. "Writing and Publishing in the Boundaries: Academic Writing in/through the Virtual Age." *The Writing Instructor* 2002. 22 September 2008 <http://www.writinginstructor.com/essays/webb.html>

Roen, Duane H., Stuart C. Brown, and Theresa Enos, eds. *Living Rhetoric and Composition: Stories of the Discipline.* Mahwah, NJ: Lawrence Erlbaum, 1999.

Smallwood, Carol, ed. *Educators as Writers: Publishing for Personal and Professional Development.* New York: Peter Lang, 2006.

Welch, Nancy, Catherine G. Latterell, Cindy Moore, and Sheila Carter-Tod, eds. *The Dissertation and the Discipline: Reinventing Composition Studies.* Portsmouth, NH: Boynton/Cook-Heinemann, 2002.

Appendix A: Assessing Your Library Resources

This appendix will help you to identify and evaluate the library resources at your disposal for bibliographic research in composition studies. The questions that follow are grouped to help you assess resources you can use at your university's library, at other academic libraries near you, and at public libraries where you have borrowing privileges. Try to answer as many of the questions as possible using only the online websites for these libraries so that you can better determine the extent to which library resources and services are available electronically.

Questions About Your University's Library

1. What is your university library's website address? If a quick link to the library's site is not provided on your university's homepage, you may want to bookmark the library's website on the computer you use most often so you can find it more conveniently. Take several minutes to explore the library's website. What sorts of information does the site provide?

2. Where on campus is the library located? Large universities may have several library buildings, so be sure you locate the one where books and journals in composition studies are housed. What hours is the library open? The hours are likely to be posted on the library's website, but because the hours may change during an academic term—reduced hours during holidays and perhaps increased hours during exam periods—be aware that you may need to check the website again to note possible changes to these hours.

3. If your library shelves books using the Library of Congress classification system, the books related to composition studies

will be shelved in the vicinity of the call number PE1404. If your library instead shelves books using the Dewey Decimal classification system, the books related to composition studies will be shelved in the vicinity of the call number 808.04207. Which classification system for shelving books does your university library use? Where in the library are the composition studies books shelved (on what floor and in what general area of that floor)? Does your library's online catalog indicate whether a book is available or checked out?

4. You can reasonably predict the size of your library's book holdings in composition studies if you know the history and size of degree programs that are related to composition studies at your university. Institutions that offer a doctoral program related to composition studies are likely to have a larger collection of relevant scholarly sources than institutions that offer only a master's degree in the field. Graduate programs in composition studies that have larger student enrollments and/or that have existed for many years are likely to be supported by more extensive library holdings in the field than graduate programs that have smaller student enrollments and/or that have been initiated more recently. Based on the degree programs in composition studies at your university, how large do you expect the library's book collection in composition studies to be? Next, scan the shelves containing books related to composition studies when you are in the library or search the call number above in the library's online catalog and then scan the holdings. Is the collection of books related to composition studies at your university's library larger or smaller than you expected?

5. Libraries generally shelve all journals together on one floor or sometimes in an area called the "Stacks." Some libraries shelve journals alphabetically (which is advantageous because the journals are then easy to find without call numbers), while other libraries shelve journals by call number (which is advantageous because then journals in the same field are near each other). Be aware that if journals are shelved alphabetically, the volumes of journals that undergo name changes may not be shelved together. For example, at my own university library, which shelves journals alphabetically, *Journal of Advanced Composition* is lo-

cated in one location through volume 15, but then is shelved in a different location beginning with volume 16 because the journal's name changed to *JAC: A Journal of Composition Theory.* Where are the journals in your library located? What method of organizing journals does your library use? Will you need a call number to find a particular journal?

6. Journal articles play a more vital role in composition studies than they do in many other humanities fields, so you are fortunate if your library has a generous collection of the field's journals. Using your library's online catalog, complete the table provided in Appendix D so that you will have a handy guide to the volumes of key journals in composition studies that are owned by your library. Whenever you identify a promising journal article citation in a bibliography or database, you can then consult this table to quickly ascertain whether your library owns the journal and volume you need. (If you are doing this library analysis as part of a class, the completion of Appendix D is a task especially well suited for several students to share.)

7. Although a few of the databases that are essential to bibliographic research in composition studies are open access, available on the internet to any user, many databases charge a hefty subscription fee and are only available to the patrons of libraries who pay for these databases. On your library's website, locate a list of the databases available through your university's library. The following subscription-based databases are useful because they most thoroughly index scholarly publications in composition studies: ERIC, JSTOR, *MLA International Bibliography*, and WorldCat. Does your university's library subscribe to them all? The following general databases can also be useful because they index some journals in composition studies that are not indexed elsewhere or because they provide online, full-text copies of articles in some composition studies journals: Academic Search Premier, Periodical Abstracts (perhaps abbreviated as PerAbs), ProQuest Research Library, and Wilson Select Plus. Which of these databases are available through your library? If your research topic is interdisciplinary, what databases are offered by your library that index scholarly sources in the disciplines that impact your research topic? Finally, does your library list among

its online databases *Ulrich's Periodicals Directory*, a reference for learning more about individual scholarly journals?

8. Most academic libraries provide their students, faculty, and staff with online access to the library's databases so that the databases can be used outside of the library. To determine how your library arranges this access, look on your library's website for information about off-campus access, a proxy server, or a VPN (virtual private network). How can your library's databases be accessed from a remote location? What patron information is needed to access these databases remotely?

9. If you need a book that is not available from your own campus library, you can use your library's interlibrary loan services to locate the book at another library and to have it shipped to your own university's library so you can borrow it. There is likely to be a link on your university library's website that explains your interlibrary loan options in more detail. A strong interlibrary loan service is one that allows you to borrow from a large number of libraries (thereby increasing the likelihood that the source you need will be available), while also encouraging the use of libraries that are closest to you (thereby reducing the length of time it takes for the source you request to arrive). Some libraries have more than one interlibrary loan system. For example, my own institution, located in Chicago, is part of a 65-library consortium of academic and research libraries in Illinois. Interlibrary loan requests are filled through this consortium first, and then only if a book is not available through one of these libraries is the library patron directed to a second interlibrary loan service, which uses a different form to request the book from a more distant library. What are the procedures at your university's library for requesting a book through interlibrary loan? How extensive is the list of libraries from which you can borrow? Can the interlibrary loan request be submitted online? What information is needed to complete this request? What is the estimated delivery time for this service? Can you check on the status of your request and if so, how? How will you be alerted when a book you have requested arrives? Be aware that the loan period for books borrowed through interlibrary loan is usually determined by the lending library and may

therefore differ from the loan period for books borrowed from your own library.

10. Can you obtain copies of journal articles through interlibrary loan, and if so, how can a request be submitted? Is there a fee for this service? What information about the article is required for you to submit the request? For example, at my own institution, patrons are required not only to provide the full citation for the article but also to indicate what database was used to locate the article's citation. How long is it likely to take to fill your request for an article? How will the article be delivered to you: as a hard copy for you to pick up or as a scanned text emailed to you electronically? How will you be alerted that the article is available? Is it possible to check on the status of your request, and if so, how?

11. Can you access a record of your library account online? If so, does the record indicate what sources you have checked out from both your own library and other libraries you may have used through interlibrary loan? Are the due dates for books indicated on this online record? Can you renew materials online?

12. Some bibliographic research tasks can be done online, such as using catalogs to find books, using databases to find journal articles and other sources, and requesting sources through interlibrary loan. Other bibliographic research tasks must be done on the library's premises, such as checking out books, photocopying journal articles that you are unable to find as full text online, and picking up books you have requested through interlibrary loan. What other bibliographic research tasks can you think of that can be completed at your university using online services? What other tasks must be completed at your university on the library premises?

Questions About Other Academic Libraries

1. In addition to the library at the university you are attending, there may be other academic libraries that you are allowed to use. Often, academic libraries have reciprocal borrowing arrangements with other colleges and universities in the nearby area, giving students at these schools access to each other's li-

braries (this is particularly true for public institutions). If you are a graduate student who attended a different institution as an undergraduate, you may still have access to your alma mater's library, especially if you are a member of that school's alumni association. After referring to the library websites of your own university and other institutions, make a list of the academic libraries that you are allowed to enter and that you could travel to, if necessary, while working on a bibliographic research project.

2. Using the institutional websites for these colleges and universities, identify which of these schools (if any) offer a graduate degree related to composition studies. Those that do are most likely to have in their library holdings the books and journals that are useful to your research.

3. Because books are usually easily obtained through interlibrary loan services, the primary benefit of having physical access to other libraries is so you can copy journal articles and use databases that are not available at your own library. Identify one academic library besides the one at your own university that you would consider visiting in person. What documentation must you present to gain entry to this library? Some possible documentation requirements include your identification card from your own university, a special borrower's card, or a letter from your own university's library. If you are permitted access to this library, what hours is it open, according to the library's website?

4. Does your library participate in a reciprocal borrowing program, enabling you to check out books from that library using your own student identification card? If so, must you return any books you borrow in person or can you return them through your own library's interlibrary loan service? Does that university library's catalogue indicate whether books it owns are available or checked out?

5. Does the alternate library you are investigating own any journals in Appendix D that are not owned by your own library? If your own university's subscription to any journals in Appendix D is incomplete, does this library own earlier or more recent

volumes of those journals? You can answer these questions using the library's catalog on its website.

6. In the first section of this appendix about resources at your own university, question seven asked you to determine whether the databases most useful to bibliographic research in composition studies are available at your own university's library. Does the academic library you are now investigating subscribe to any helpful databases that are not available at your own library? If so, the databases may not be available remotely except to those enrolled at that university, but often computers that are inside a library are programmed so that anyone inside the library can use them without entering their patron identification. If you want to use a database available at this library that is not available at your own library, you can call the library to ask whether you will be able to access the database from the library premises without logging in. Most librarians are so pleased to find savvy library users eager for resources that they will answer you honestly and overlook this loophole in gaining database access.

Questions About Public Libraries

1. If you are attending school in a different geographic area from where you normally reside, determine whether you can obtain public library cards from both your hometown and the city where you attend school. Although public libraries are generally ill-equipped for scholarly research, a well-funded public library may subscribe to a useful database that your university library lacks. For what public libraries do you already have a library card? Are there additional public libraries for which you can obtain a card?

2. While working on this book, I discovered that full-text copies of articles from several composition journals (including *English Journal, Journal of Basic Writing, Issues in Writing,* and *Rhetorica*) are available through a commercial database named ProQuest Research. My campus library does not subscribe to this database; however, the Chicago Public Library does subscribe to it. Because I am a Chicago resident with a Chicago Public Library card, I can log in to the ProQuest Research da-

tabase through the Chicago Public Library website, using my public library card identification number, and can conveniently obtain the full text of many articles from these journals in composition studies. To test whether a similar scenario is possible for you, consult the websites of public libraries you can access to identify the databases available to patrons. Do the public libraries you are allowed to access subscribe to any useful databases that are not available at your own university? Can you use these databases remotely by entering your patron identification? After scanning the final lines of the journal descriptions in Appendix B, list the journals in composition studies that can be accessed using these additional databases.

Appendix B: Scholarly Journals in Composition

Note: The circulation numbers for journals in this appendix were gathered in 2007 from the "Directory of Periodicals" in *MLA International Bibliography* (online version), from *Magazines for Libraries* (15th edition), and from *Ulrich's Periodicals Directory* (online version). For some journals, the circulation numbers differed greatly in these reference guides. In those instances, the circulation reported is an average of the circulation figures in those guides.

Across the Disciplines

The full title of this open access, electronic journal is *Across the Disciplines: Interdisciplinary Perspectives on Language, Learning, and Academic Writing.* The journal began in 2004 and is the result of a merger of two prior journals: Language and Learning Across the Disciplines (a print journal issued 1994–2003) and *Academic Writing* (an online journal issued 2000–2003). According to its website, http://wac.colostate.edu/atd/, the journal provides "a venue for scholarly debate about issues of disciplinarity and writing across the curriculum." Rather than having regularly scheduled issues, each year's volume evolves as refereed articles are accepted and published online. The full texts of all articles, as well as the full texts of articles from the two previous periodicals, are available at the journal's website. The website offers a search function, and articles are also indexed in *MLA International Bibliography.*

Assessing Writing: An International Journal

This journal is published three times a year and began in 1994. As stated in *Ulrich's Periodicals Directory,* the journal "explores writing assessment issues from diverse perspectives: classrooms, research, institutional, and administrative." Topics include testing, portfolios, classroom assessment, technology-assisted assessment, the assessment of writing done in non-educational settings, and international perspectives on writing assessment, among others. The tables of contents for all issues (including the most recent) and abstracts for all articles are available at this site: http://www.sciencedirect.com/science/journal/10752935. This site may also be used to search the journal by keyword and to obtain full texts of any article (free to subscribers of the journal or available for purchase to non-subscribers).

College Composition and Communication

This journal (commonly abbreviated as *CCC*) is published four times a year and began in 1950. It is published by the National Council of Teachers of English (NCTE) and is the primary journal for college writing teachers, with a circulation of approximately 10,000. As stated in *Ulrich's Periodicals Directory,* the journal "contains articles dealing with the theory, practice, [and] research of composition, and the preparation of writing teachers."

The tables of contents for all issues since 1997 (including the most recent issues) and abstracts for all of the articles published during these years are available at this site: http://www.ncte.org/cccc/ccc/issues. Subscribers of the journal can retrieve full text of these articles online for free at this site, and non-subscribers can use the site to purchase a copy of any issue. Although the NCTE site is not searchable by keyword, this journal may be searched by keyword using the *CCC Online Archive,* available at http://www.inventio.us/ccc/. The issues included in this archive are those published since 1987 (including the most recent issues). Again, abstracts of the articles are available to all, but full texts are available only to subscribers of the journal. A unique feature of this site is that a "reversible" bibliography is provided for each article, listing not only the works cited in an article but also any *CCC* article published later that cites that article.

If your library subscribes to JSTOR, the best way to search for *CCC* articles is to use JSTOR to find articles prior to the last three complete years. You can then save and print the exact page images of articles, which are helpful whenever you quote from an article and need to cite the page number on which that quote appears. Then use the *CCC Online Archive* site to search more recent volumes, as well as to examine the reversible bibliography of any earlier *CCC* article that is especially important to your research project.

College English

This journal (commonly abbreviated as *CE*) is published every two months and began in 1939. It is published by the National Council of Teachers of English (NCTE) and is a prominent journal for college English teachers, with a circulation of approximately 12,000. As stated in *Ulrich's Periodicals Directory,* the journal "examines various study and teaching methods for teachers of college-level English language arts." The journal's articles pertain to literature, composition studies, critical theory, linguistics, pedagogy, and professional issues related to the teaching of English.

The tables of contents for all issues since 1997 (including the most recent issues) and abstracts for all of the articles published during these years are available at this site: http://www.ncte.org/journals/ce/issues. Subscribers of the journal can use this site to read the full text of these articles online for free, and non-subscribers may use the site to purchase a copy of any issue. The site is not searchable by keyword.

If your library subscribes to JSTOR, the best way to search for *College English* articles is to use JSTOR to find articles published prior to the last three complete years so that you can save and print exact pages images of the article. Keyword searches and the full text of articles published more recently than those included in JSTOR—often as recent as the latest issue—are available through your library's subscription to the database Periodical Abstracts or to the database ProQuest Research Library.

Community Literacy Journal

This journal is published twice a year and began in 2006. According to its website, http://www.communityliteracy.org, the journal is concerned with "literacy work that exists outside mainstream educational and work institutions." The website offers tables of contents for all issues, abstract of all articles, and a search function. Full texts of articles are available through delayed open access on the site twenty-four months after their publication. The journal is not currently indexed.

Composition Studies

This journal was originally published as *Freshman English News* (or *FEN*) in 1972–1991. It was then renamed to *Composition Studies* in 1992 and has since been published twice a year, with a circulation of approximately 1,000. As stated in *Ulrich's Periodicals Directory*, the journal "publishes essays on theories of composition and rhetoric, the teaching and administration of writing and rhetoric at all post-secondary levels, and disciplinary-institutional issues of interest to the field's teacher-scholars." A course design, including the course rationale, syllabus and schedule, is also published in each issue.

The journal's website is http://www.compositionstudies.tcu.edu. The website provides the tables of contents of all issues published since the journal's name change in 1992, as well as abstracts of select articles in each issue. The site also provides a cumulative list of all articles published in *Freshman English News*, 1972–1991, although no abstracts are provided of these articles. The site is searchable by keyword. Your library may have a subscription to the Academic Search Premier database, which provides full texts of *Composition Studies* articles published since 2004.

Computers and Composition: An International Journal

This journal is published four times a year, began in 1983, and has a circulation of approximately 600. As stated in *Ulrich's Periodicals Directory*, the journal "includes information on subjects related to computer use in composition classrooms and programs."

The journal's website is http://www.computersandcomposition. osu.edu. The "resources" link on this site offers an extensive bibliography of sources related to computers and composition, including but not restricted to articles published in the journal. With the exception of the journal's first two volumes, the tables of contents for all issues (including the most recent) and abstracts for all articles are available at this site: http://www.sciencedirect.com/science/journal/87554615. This site may also be used to search the journal by keyword and to obtain full texts of any article (free to subscribers of the journal or available for purchase to non-subscribers).

Enculturation

The full title of this refereed, open access online journal is *Enculturation: A Journal for Rhetoric, Writing, and Culture*. It is issued twice a year and began in 1997. Its website, http://enculturation.gmu.edu, describes the journal as "devoted to contemporary theorizations of rhetoric, writing, and culture." Many issues have special themes, such as electronic publishing, visual rhetoric, or post-digital studies. Full texts of all articles are available on the website. The website offers a search function, and the journal is indexed in *MLA International Bibliography*.

English Journal

This journal is published every two months, began in 1912, and has a circulation of approximately 51,000. It is published by the National Council of Teachers of English (NCTE) and is a primary journal for teachers of English in middle schools, junior high schools, and high schools. As stated in *Ulrich's Periodicals Directory*, the journal "allows for middle- and high-school English teachers to explore important issues in teaching language arts and literature." The articles in each journal issue address a common theme, such a teaching grammar or teaching in urban schools.

The tables of contents for all issues since 1996 (including the most recent issues) and abstracts for all of the articles published during these years are available at this site: http://www.ncte.org/journals/ej/issues. Subscribers of the journal can use this site to read the full text of articles online for free, and non-subscribers may use the site to purchase a copy of any issue. The site is not searchable by keyword.

If your library subscribes to JSTOR, the best way to search for *English Journal* articles is to use JSTOR to find articles published prior to the last three complete years because the exact page images are most helpful when a page citation is needed to quote from an article. Keyword searches and the full text of articles published more recently than those included in JSTOR—often as recent as the latest issue—are available through your library's subscription to the database Periodical Abstracts or to the database ProQuest Research Library.

Issues in Writing

The full title of this journal is *Issues in Writing: Education, Government, Arts and Humanities, Business and Industry, Science and Technology*.

The journal is published twice a year, began in 1988, and has a circulation of approximately 150. According to its website, the journal aims "to encourage discussion of writing in ways that cut across disciplines, definitions, and traditional boundaries." Articles are written by academics in all disciplines and by professionals with non-academic careers. The journal's website, http://www.uwsp.edu/english/iw/, offers tables of contents and abstracts of articles published in all issues. The website offers a search function, and the journal is also indexed in *MLA International Bibliography*. Full texts of articles are available through your library's subscription to the database Wilson Select Plus (2001–2004) or to the database ProQuest Research Library (2003 to present).

JAC: A Journal of Composition Theory

This journal began in 1979 and was originally published once a year under the title *Journal of Advanced Composition*. In 1990, it began to be published twice a year, and it changed to its current name in 2002. The journal's circulation is approximately 1,000. As stated in *Ulrich's Periodicals Directory*, the journal "publishes theoretical articles on a variety of topics related to rhetoric, writing, multiple literacies, and the politics of education." The journal's website, http://www.jacweb.org, indicates a commitment to make all but the three most recent issues available as full texts on the website. A chart on the website indicates the current progress of these electronic archives. The site also provides a Google search feature. The journal can also be searched using *MLA International Bibliography*.

Journal of Basic Writing

This journal is published twice a year, began in 1978, and has a circulation of approximately 1,400. The articles published in this journal discuss the theory and teaching of basic writing and English as a second language (ESL). The journal's website is http://orgs.tamu-commerce.edu/cbw/cbw/JBW.html. The archives link provides the authors, titles, and abstracts of all articles published from volume 15 (1996) to 26 (2007), but it does not provide the page numbers of the articles necessary for citations and does not currently provide information on recent issues. Also, the website has no search capacities. In addition to searching the journal using ERIC and *MLA International Bibliography*, the journal is indexed in the database Periodical Abstracts beginning with the 2005 volume, although full text is available for 2005 only. The full text of articles published from 2004 to the present is available if your library subscribes to the database ProQuest Research Library.

Journal of Business Communication

This journal publishes four issues per year, began in 1963, and has a circulation of approximately 1,875. The journal's articles address business communication, including such topics as management communication, information systems, international business communication, and organizational and corporate communication, among others. A more detailed description of the journal is available at its website: http://www.businesscommunication.org/publications/jbc/about_jbc. html. For archives of the journal that are searchable by keyword, consult http://job.sagepub.com/archive/, where you'll find tables of contents for all issues (including the most recent), abstracts for all articles since 1967, and full text available free of charge to subscribers of the journal and available for purchase to non-subscribers. Additionally, full text is available through your library's subscription to the Wilson Select Plus database for the years 1998–2002 only.

Journal of Business and Technical Communication

This journal is published four times a year, began in 1987, and has a circulation of approximately 400. As stated in *Ulrich's Periodicals Directory,* the journal "provides information on the latest communication practices, problems, and trends in both industry and the academic world." Articles focus on writing for businesses and professions, sciences, and government. The journal's readers include academics and professionals in industry. At the website http://jbt.sagepub.com/ archive/, there are tables of contents and abstracts for all issues, as well as full text provided free of charge to subscribers of the journal or available for purchase to non-subscribers. The website offers both basic and advanced search functions. The full text of articles published in 1996–1998 only is available through your library's subscription to Periodical Abstracts.

Journal of Second Language Writing

This journal is published four times a year, began in 1992, and has a circulation of approximately 400. As stated in *Ulrich's Periodicals*

Directory, the journal "publishes theoretically grounded reports of research and discussions of central issues in second and foreign language writing and writing instruction." Each issue also includes an annotated bibliography of recent scholarship in second language writing.

The website http://www.jslw.org/ provides more information about the journal, tables of contents for all issues, and a search capacity. These features, along with abstracts of all articles (available to all) and full texts of all articles (free to subscribers of the journal and available for purchase to non-subscribers), are also available at http://www.sciencedirect.com/science/journal/10603743.

Journal of Teaching Writing

This journal is published twice a year and began in 1982. As stated in *Ulrich's Periodicals Directory,* the journal "publishes articles on the theory, practice, and teaching of writing throughout the curriculum. [It] covers a range of topics from composition theory and discourse analysis to curriculum development and innovative teaching techniques." Its audience is those who teach writing at all levels, from preschool through university, who are interested in pedagogical practice. The journal's website, http://www.iupui.edu/~jtw/, is not searchable by keyword, but it lists all of the articles published in the journal until 2004, organized by issue and alphabetically by the authors' names. If your university has a subscription to the journal as well as to the Electronic Journals Online database, you can access full text articles published in 2004 or later through that database.

Journal of Technical Writing and Communication

This journal is published four times a year and began in 1971. As stated in *Ulrich's Periodicals Directory,* the journal "contains essays on oral, as well as written communication, for purposes from pure research to needs of business and industry." Its intended audience is teachers and practitioners of technical and scientific writing. Its website, http://baywood.com/journals/PreviewJournals.asp?Id=0047–2816, is searchable by keyword, and tables of contents and article abstracts are available for all issues. The full text of articles is available online (free of charge to journal subscribers and available for purchase to non-subscribers).

Kairos: A Journal for Teachers of Writing and Webbed Environments

This journal is published three times a year, began in 1996, and is an open access online journal. Its articles explore the intersections of rhetoric, technology, and pedagogy within higher education. The articles in each issue address a common theme, and the electronic journal is fully searchable. The full text of all issues is available at the journal's website: http://kairos.technorhetoric.net.

KB Journal

This journal began in 2004, is published twice a year (in the fall and spring), and is an open access online journal. According to its website, located at http://www.kbjournal.org, *KB Journal* "publishes original scholarship that addresses, applies, repurposes, or challenges the teachings of Kenneth Burke." In addition to full text articles of all issues, the website offers basic and advanced search functions (click the "Search KB" tab), bibliographies of works by and about Burke, and a Burke discussion list. Beginning with the 2005 issues, the journal is indexed in the *MLA International Bibliography*.

Philosophy and Rhetoric

This journal is published four times a year, began in 1968, and has a circulation of approximately 700. As stated in *Ulrich's Periodicals Directory*, the journal "publishes articles on the relations between philosophy and rhetoric," including logic and argumentation. The journal's editorial board is composed half of philosophers and half of specialists in Speech, English, and the Classics, which reflects the multi-disciplinary nature of the journal. A fuller description of the journal is available at its website, http://www.psupress.org/journals/jnls_pr.html. To see the tables of contents of all issues since 1999, consult this website: http://www.press.jhu.edu/journals/philosophy_and_rhetoric. The full texts of all issues since 2000 are available online if your library subscribes to the databases Project Muse Premium Collection or OCLC FirstSearch's ECO (Electronic Collection Online).

Pre/Text

This journal is published four times a year, began in 1979, and has a circulation of approximately 600. As stated in *Ulrich's Periodicals Directory*, the journal "covers [the] wide broadly conceived area of

Rhetorical Theory." Its articles also address pedagogical philosophy. Without a journal subscription, its archives are not easily accessible because it is not indexed and its website, http://www.pre-text.com, indicates that the journal has not ceased production but is several years behind schedule.

Reflections: A Journal of Writing, Service-Learning, and Community Literacy

This journal began in 2000 and publishes issues twice a year. Its articles address service-learning, community-based writing and civic engagement. Its website, http://www.reflectionsjournal.org, provides the tables of contents and abstracts of all volumes, as well as a search function. The journal is not indexed, but full texts of any article can be purchased and downloaded from the journal's website for the nominal cost of one dollar each.

Research in the Teaching of English

This journal is published four times a year, began in 1967, and has a circulation of 4,100. Published by the National Council of Teachers of English (NCTE), the journal includes empirical research reports on literacy issues, preschool through adult, as well as essays on research methodology. Beginning in 1967, the journal published a selective bibliography of published research in composition studies twice a year, in every May and November issue, and those bibliographies were annotated beginning in May 1973. In 2004, the bibliography in *RTE* became annual, published each November with selected sources annotated and a more extensive list of relevant citations that are not annotated.

The tables of contents for all issues since 1997 (including the most recent issues) and abstracts for all of the articles published during these years are available at this site: http://www.ncte.org/journals/rte/issues. Subscribers of the journal can retrieve the full texts of these articles online for free at this site, and non-subscribers can use the site to purchase a copy of any issue. Although the NCTE site is not searchable by keyword, all but the first three years and last few years can be searched using ERIC.

Rhetoric Review

This journal is published four times a year, began in 1982, and has a circulation of approximately 1,250. According to its website, the journal "publishes manuscripts that explore the breadth and depth of the discipline, including history, theory, writing, praxis, technical/professional communication, philosophy, rhetorical criticism, cultural studies, multiple literacies, technology, literature, public address, graduate education, and professional issues." The journal's website, http://www.rhetoricreview.com/, provides more information about the journal.

If your library subscribes to JSTOR, the best way to search for *Rhetoric Review* articles is to use JSTOR to find articles published prior to the last five complete years because the exact page images are most helpful when a page citation is needed to quote from an article. Keyword searches and the full text of articles published more recently than those included in JSTOR are available through your library's subscription to Academic Search Premier (full text 2001–present with a 12-month delay) or through the site http://www.leaonline.com/loi/rr (full text 2001–present provided free to subscribers of the journal and available for purchase to non-subscribers).

Rhetoric Society Quarterly

This journal is published four times a year, began in 1968, and has a circulation of approximately 700. It is published by the Rhetoric Society of America, a multi-disciplinary organization of rhetoricians in communication, composition, English, history, philosophy, politics, speech, and other related fields. As stated in *Ulrich's Periodicals Directory,* the journal "covers topics relating to the history, theory, criticism and pedagogy of rhetoric."

If your library subscribes to JSTOR, the best way to search for *Rhetoric Society Quarterly* articles is to use JSTOR to find articles published prior to the last seven complete years because the exact page images are most helpful when a page citation is needed to quote from an article. Keyword searches and the full text of articles published more recently than those included in JSTOR are available through your library's subscriptions to ProQuest Research Library (2004 to present) and Periodical Abstracts (2005 to present). Also, the journal's website, http://rhetoricsociety.org/, provides the tables of contents and abstracts for all articles published since 2002 and offers both basic and advanced search functions.

Rhetorica: A Journal of the History of Rhetoric

This journal is published four times a year, began in 1983, and has a circulation of approximately 1,000. It is published by the International Society for the History of Rhetoric. As stated in *Ulrich's Periodicals Directory*, the journal "examines the theory, practice, and cultural context of rhetoric." More information about the journal is available at its website, http://www.ucpressjournals.com/journalSoc.asp?j=rh. If your library subscribes to JSTOR, the best way to search for *Rhetorica* articles is to use JSTOR to find articles published prior to the last three years because the exact page images are most helpful when a page citation is needed to quote from from an article. The journal is also indexed in the *MLA International Bibliography* and in Academic Search Premier (2000 to present), and full texts of the articles published since 2002 can be obtained if your library subscribes to ProQuest Research Library.

Teaching English in the Two-Year College

This journal is issued four times a year, began in 1974, and has a circulation of approximately 4,200. As stated in *Ulrich's Periodicals Directory*, the journal "publishes theoretical and practical articles on composition, developmental studies, technical and business communication, literature, creative expression, language, and the profession." It is published by the National Council of Teachers of English (NCTE), and its intended audience is teachers of English in two-year colleges, as well as teachers of first- and second-year writing courses in four-year colleges and universities.

The tables of contents for all issues since 1996 (including the most recent issues) and abstracts for all of the articles published during these years are available at this site: www.ncte.org/journals/tetyc/issues. Subscribers to the journal can retrieve the full text of these articles online for free at this site, and non-subscribers can use the site to purchase a copy of any issue. The NCTE site is not searchable by keyword.

Technical Communication

The full title of this journal is *Technical Communication: Journal for the Society of Technical Communication*. The journal is issued four times a year, began in 1953, and has a circulation of approximately 21,000. Its articles address practical applications of technical communication theory. Major articles are published under the headings "Applied Theory," "Case History," "Review of Research," "Tutorials," "The Practice," and "Global Perspectives." The website http://www.stc.org/pubs/techcom-mGeneral01.asp provides a brief description of the journal.

In addition to ERIC, the journal is indexed in Periodical Abstracts (with full texts 1994–2005) and ProQuest Research Library (with full texts 1994–2005). Abstracts of all articles published since 1995 and the full texts of these articles (free to subscribers and available for purchase by non-subscribers) are available at http://www.ingentaconnect.com/content/stc/tc, although this site is not searchable by keyword.

Technical Communication Quarterly

This journal is published four times a year and has a circulation of 1,500. Published by the Association of Teachers of Technical Writing (ATTW), it began in 1973 under the journal name *Technical Writing Teacher* and assumed its current name in 1992. According to the journal's website, http://cms.english.ttu.edu/attw/tcq, "all articles have a sound basis in theory, use accessible examples and illustrations, and include implications for teaching, research, or practice in technical communication."

In addition to being indexed in ERIC and *MLA International Bibliography*, the journal is indexed in Academic Search Premier (1998–present), Wilson Select Plus (full text 2000–2005), and Periodical Abstracts (full text 2002–2006). Tables of contents, abstracts, and full texts (free to journal subscribers and available for purchase to non-subscribers) are also available at http://www.leaonline.com/loi/tcq (1996–1997 and 2001–present issue).

TESOL Quarterly

This journal is published four times a year, began in 1967, and has a circulation of approximately 12,000. It publishes articles on teaching and research in English as a second language. Each September issue is devoted to articles about a special topic. The TESOL website, http://www.tesol.org/s_tesol/index.asp, provides more information about the journal, as well as other TESOL resources, and subscribers of the journal only can access full text articles online through this site.

If your library subscribes to JSTOR, the best way to search for *TESOL Quarterly* articles is to use JSTOR to find articles published prior to the last five complete years because the exact page images are most helpful when you quote from an article and need to cite the page number. Keyword searches of articles published more recently than those included in JSTOR are available through *MLA International Bibliography*, and full texts of articles published since 2001 are available if your library subscribes to the database Ingenta.

The WAC Journal

This journal is published annually in September (with approximately 120 pages per volume) and began in 1989. The first eleven volumes of this journal were published under the title *The Plymouth State University Journal on Writing Across the Curriculum*. Volume 12 was a transitional volume that included authors from other institutions, and beginning with volume 13, the journal assumed its current name and became a national, refereed periodical. Its articles address the practice and theory of writing across the curriculum. The journal's website, http://wac.colostate.edu/journal/, includes the full text of all issues in Adobe Acrobat PDF. The journal is not indexed in a periodicals database, but the website provides a Google search function.

WPA: Writing Program Administration

This journal of the Council of Writing Program Administrators is published twice a year, began in 1977, and has a circulation of approximately 600. As stated in *Ulrich's Periodicals Directory*, the journal "deals with [the] administration of college and university writing programs: theory, research, and professional practices." The journal's website is http://wpa-council.org. It is indexed in ERIC (1987, 1989–1994, 1997–2001) and in *MLA International Bibliography*; full texts are available online. Only WPA members can access issues published in the last three years. All others are available in PDF format.

The Writing Center Journal

This journal is published twice a year, began in 1980, and has a circulation of approximately 1,000. As stated in *Ulrich's Periodicals Directory*, the journal "publishes articles, reviews, and announcements to writing center personnel, particularly manuscripts that explore issues or theories related to writing center dynamics or administration." The journal's website, http://www.ou.edu/wcj/, contains the full texts of articles published 1980–2004 and the tables of contents for articles from 2005 until two years ago, though it does not have a search function. Abstracts of all articles published prior to 2000 appear in Volume 20.2 of the journal, available on the site. The journal is also indexed in ERIC (1984, 1986–2003) and in *MLA International Bibliography*.

The Writing Instructor

This journal began in 1981 and became an open access online journal in 2001, with articles added irregularly. Its articles focus on writing pedagogy, research, and theory in K-12 schools and in higher education. Its website, http://www.writinginstructor.com, has a search function and provides full text articles of all issues since 2001. The journal is indexed in ERIC (1983–1985, 1987–1997), *MLA International Bibliography*, Wilson Select Plus (full text 1996–1997 only), and ProQuest Research Library (full text 1996–1997 only).

Writing Lab Newsletter

This refereed newsletter is issued ten times a year (monthly from September through June), began in 1977, and has a circulation of approximately 1,000. As stated on the journal's website, "articles focus on challenges in tutoring theory and methodology, handling ESL issues, directing a writing center, training tutors, adding computers, designing and expanding centers, and using tutorial theory and pedagogy." The website has recently added a keyword search function, and full texts of all issues except the current year are available as PDF files on the website http://writinglabnewsletter.org/.

Writing on the Edge

The full title of this journal is *Writing on the Edge: A Journal about Writing and Teaching Writing*. The journal is published twice a year and began in 1989. It publishes scholarly articles that veer from traditional academic forms, especially articles concerning student diversity and new approaches to teaching college-level composition. Its website, http://woe.ucdavis.edu, contains the tables of contents of all issues, but it has no page numbers, abstracts, or full texts and is not searchable. The journal is not indexed elsewhere.

Written Communication

This journal's full title is *Written Communication: An International Quarterly of Research, Theory, and Application*. It is published four times a year, began in 1984, and has a circulation of approximately 1,350. As stated in *Ulrich's Periodicals Directory,* the journal "provides a forum for ideas, theoretical viewpoints, and methodological approaches that better define and further develop thought and practice in the study of the written word." Along with the journal *Research in the Teaching of English,* this journal is one of the major publishers of article-length reports of empirical studies in composition. The website http://wcx.sage-pub.com provides the tables of contents and abstracts for all articles published in the journal, as well as full texts provided free to subscribers of the journal and available for purchase to non-subscribers. The website also offers both basic and advanced search functions.

Appendix C: Inclusion of Composition Journals in Periodical Indexes

Note: This table was accurate when created in May 2009. The journals that are indexed and the dates included may now be somewhat different. Use this table as a guide, but check the websites of the periodical indexes if you wish to update the coverage represented here.

Journal Title[1]	ERIC[2]	MLA[3]	JSTOR[4]
Across the Disciplines	No	Yes	No
Assessing Writing	Comprehensively since 1994	Yes	No
College Composition and Communication	Comprehensively since 1969	Yes	Full text from Vol. 1 in 1950 (3 year moving wall)
College English	Comprehensively since 1969	Yes	Full text from Vol. 1 in 1939 (3 year moving wall)
Community Literacy Journal	No	No	No
Composition Studies	Comprehensively since 1999	Yes	No
Computers and Composition	Selectively, 1987–2003	Yes	No
Enculturation	No	Yes	No
English Journal	Comprehensively since 1970	Yes	Full text from Vol. 1 in 1912 (3 year moving wall)
Issues in Writing	No	Yes	No

Journal Title[1]	ERIC[2]	MLA[3]	JSTOR[4]
JAC: A Journal of Composition Theory	No	Yes	No
Journal of Basic Writing	Comprehensively, 1977–1980, 1982, 1984, 1986–current	Yes	No
Journal of Business Communication	Selectively, 1973–2003	No	No
Journal of Business and Technical Communication	Selectively, 1988–2002	No	No
Journal of Second Language Writing	Comprehensively, 1992–1996 and 2001–current	No	No
Journal of Teaching Writing	Comprehensively, 1984–1996 and 1998	No	No
Journal of Technical Writing and Communication	Selectively, 1989–2003	No	No
Kairos	No	Yes	No
KB Journal	No	Yes	No
Philosophy and Rhetoric	No	Yes	No
Pre/Text	No	No	No
Reflections	No	No	No
Research in the Teaching of English	Comprehensively since 1970	No	No
Rhetoric Review	Selectively, 1984–1995	Yes	Full text from Vol. 1 in 1982 (5 year moving wall)
Rhetoric Society Quarterly	Selectively, 1985–1987, 1992–1993, 1995–1996	Yes	Full text from Vol. 1 in 1976 (7 year moving wall)
Rhetorica: A Journal of the History of Rhetoric	No	Yes	Full text from Vol. 1 in 1983 (3 year moving wall)
Teaching English in the Two-Year College	Comprehensively since 1974	Yes	No
Technical Communication	Selectively, 1988, 1990–2003	No	No

Journal Title[1]	ERIC[2]	MLA[3]	JSTOR[4]
Technical Communication Quarterly	Selectively, 1992–2003	Yes	No
TESOL Quarterly	Comprehensively since 1969	Yes	Full text from Vol. 1 in 1967 (5 year moving wall)
The WAC Journal	No	No	No
WPA: Writing Program Administration	Comprehensively, 1987, 1989–1994, 1997–2001	Yes	No
The Writing Center Journal	Comprehensively, 1984, 1986–2003	Yes	No
The Writing Instructor	Comprehensively, 1983–1985, 1987–1997	Yes	No
Writing Lab Newsletter	No	Yes	No
Writing on the Edge	Selectively, 1989–1997, 2001–2003	No	No
Written Communication	Comprehensively since 1984	No	No

[1] A description of each of these journals appears in Appendix B. The descriptions also indicate additional means of obtaining abstracts and full texts of articles published in these journals, besides the three indexes featured here.

[2] If a journal is indexed comprehensively in ERIC, all articles in these issues are included. If a journal is indexed selectively, only education-related articles in these issues are indexed. The most recent issues are not likely to be included; you can verify the exact years of coverage by consulting http://www.eric.ed.gov and clicking on "Journals Indexed in ERIC."

[3] *MLA International Bibliography* does not provide detailed information about the inclusive dates that any journal is indexed. "Yes" indicates simply that MLA states that this journal is "actively indexed"; "no" indicates that MLA does not actively index this journal.

[4] JSTOR indexes its journals beginning with the first volume of each. The moving wall indicates the length of the delay before recent issues are included; partial years are not counted when calculating the moving wall.

Appendix D: Journals Holdings in Nearby Libraries

Journal Title	Volumes owned by campus library	Alternate library or online source	Call number (if needed)
Across the Disciplines	Open access at http://wac.colostate.edu/atd		
Assessing Writing			
College Composition and Communication			
College English			
Community Literacy Journal			
Composition Studies			
Computers and Composition			

Journal Title	Volumes owned by campus library	Alternate library or online source	Call number (if needed)
Enculturation	Open access at http://enculturation.gmu.edu		
English Journal			
Issues in Writing			
JAC: A Journal of Composition Theory			
Journal of Basic Writing			
Journal of Business Communication			
Journal of Business and Technical Communication			
Journal of Second Language Writing			

Journal Title	Volumes owned by campus library	Alternate library or online source	Call number (if needed)
Journal of Teaching Writing			
Journal of Technical Writing and Communication			
Kairos	Open access at http://kairos.technorhetoric.net		
KB Journal	Open access at http://www.kbjournal.org		
Philosophy and Rhetoric			
Pre/Text			
Reflections			
Research in the Teaching of English			

Journal Title	Volumes owned by campus library	Alternate library or online source	Call number (if needed)
Rhetoric Review			
Rhetoric Society Quarterly			
Rhetorica: A Journal of the History of Rhetoric			
Teaching English in the Two-Year College			
Technical Communication			
Technical Communication Quarterly			
TESOL Quarterly			
The WAC Journal	Open access at http://wac.colostate.edu/journal		

Journal Title	Volumes owned by campus library	Alternate library or online source	Call number (if needed)
WPA: Writing Program Administration			
The Writing Center Journal			
The Writing Instructor	Open access at http://www.writinginstructor.com		
Writing Lab Newsletter			
Writing on the Edge			
Written Communication			

Index

Boolean operators, 58, 64, 66, 67, 79, 85
Borgman, Christine, 22
Breivik, Patricia Senn, 9, 20, 23
Brown, Stuart, 5, 21, 123
Bryant, Paul, 11, 13, 16, 21
Bugajski, Ken, 115, 122
Burke, Kenneth, 3-4, 21, 24, 141

Carter-Tod, Sheila, 123
Casanave, Christine Pearson, 123
case study, 29-30, 33, 118
Castner, Bruce, 23
CCCC, *see* Conference on College Composition and Communication
CCCC Bibliography of Composition and Rhetoric, 14, 97, 98, 100, 101
Chapman, David, 5, 21
citations, 12, 45-46, 72-75, 90-91, 92, 103-109, 113, 118-119; export, 79, 88, 92
citation analysis, 45-46
Clark, Irene, 115-117, 122
Coffey, Daniel, 12, 21, 43, 45-46, 55
CompFAQs, 37, 79-81, 93, 104
composition studies, 4-7, 11-20, 24-39, 42-55, 60, 63, 69, 71, 77, 102, 121-122, 125-127
CompPile, 14, 32-33, 43, 44, 45, 47, 49, 50, 53, 54, 63, 78-82, 84, 93, 94, 96, 104, 105, 106
CompPile Associates, 78
conferences, *see* professional organizations
Conference on Basic Writing, 51
Conference on College Composition and Communication (CCCC), 11, 13, 14, 22, 40, 51-53, 89, 97, 98, 100, 101
Connors, Robert, 5, 21, 46, 55

controlled vocabulary, 62
conventions, *see* professional organizations
conversation, 3-5, 19-20, 24, 54, 103, 121-122
Corbett, Edward, 18
Couture, Barbara, 123
criteria for selecting sources, 68-72, 105, 108; credibility, 28, 37, 69, 72, 108, 117; cumulative merit of sources, 71, 108; length of sources, 71, 91, 109; quantity of sources, 68-69, 108; relevance, 12, 14, 18, 49, 58, 61-62, 69-70, 80, 88, 91, 107-108, 114, 119; timeliness of sources, 70, 72, 120
criticism, *see* scholarship
critics, 25
Curzon, Susan Carol, 9, 21

databases, 28, 47, 49, 59-70, 77-94, 99, 104-107, 111-112, 127-128, 131-132; glossary, 62-64, 79, 81, 93, 104; thesaurus, 62-64, 67, 85-86, 88, 89, 93
Day, Michael, 56
dialectic, 25, 26
disciplinary knowledge, 14, 16, 24, 26, 32, 34, 38, 43, 53, 71, 99
discipline, 4-7, 11-16, 18-20, 24-25, 39, 43-44, 46-47, 121-122
dissertation indexes, 94, 105
dissertations and theses, 17, 46, 50-51, 68-69, 72, 79, 80, 85, 93, 94, 97, 105, 106, 117, 118, 120
Dobrin, Sidney, 41
documentation style, 72-75; APA, 73-75, 120; MLA, 73-75, 120

Ede, Lisa, 41
edited collections, 28, 43-45, 46, 79, 80, 106, 108
Emig, Janet, 30, 40, 118, 122

Smallwood, Carol, 123
Solomon, Amy, 76
Soven, Margaret Iris, 26, 40, 120
Spear, Karen, 45, 57
students, 5-10, 15, 19, 50, 59, 73,
    81-82, 104, 110, 113, 115-117,
    118, 122, 127, 129
Stygall, Gail, 98, 101
Suber, Peter, 47, 50, 56

Tate, Gary, 5, 21, 23, 98, 101
Taylor, Terry, 76
Taylor, Todd, 14, 98, 101, 123
truncation, 60, 66, 67

Vandenberg, Peter, 60, 75
Vandrick, Stephanie, 123

WAC Clearinghouse, 36, 41, 50-
    52, 94, 96

Walker, Charles, 75
Walvoord, Barbara, 26, 31, 41
Ward, Dane, 23
Waters, William, 123
Welch, Nancy, 123
West, Susan, 56
Wiemelt, Jeffrey, 23
Wiley, Mark, 44, 56
Williamson, Naomi, 76
Willinsky, John, 57
Wilson, Lizabeth, 9-10, 22
Witte, Stephen, 33
works cited, 99, 112, 134
WorldCat, 14, 33, 43, 77, 82-85,
    93, 94, 98, 99, 103, 104, 109,
    112, 127
writing across the curriculum, 25-
    28, 30-32, 36

About the Author

Vicki Byard is Professor of English at Northeastern Illinois University, located in Chicago, where she currently serves as the Coordinator of the First-Year Writing Program. She teaches first-year and upper-level writing courses, as well as graduate-level theory and research courses in an MA composition program. Previously, she authored the *Instructor's Resource Manual* for the first and second editions of *The Allyn & Bacon Guide to Writing*, and she is a frequent presenter at national conferences in composition studies. She received her MA and PhD in rhetoric and composition from Purdue University.

Photograph of the author by Elias Toynton.
Used by permission.

LaVergne, TN USA
05 October 2009
159861LV00003B/9/P